DOHA
TRAVEL GUIDE

The Complete Doha Experience: Your Indispensable Guide to Experiencing Qatar's Dynamic Capital

NICHOLAS Z. ANDREW

TABLE OF CONTENTS

CHAPTER FIVE............103

CHAPTER SIX 141

CHAPTER ONE

WELCOME TO DOHA

Doha, the vibrant capital city of Qatar, beckons visitors with its fascinating blend of tradition and modernity. Situated on the eastern coast of the Arabian Peninsula, Doha is a city that beautifully showcases the rich heritage and dynamic growth of the region. As you embark on your journey through this captivating destination, get ready to immerse yourself in a world where Arabian traditions seamlessly coexist with the luxuries of a modern metropolis.

Doha's allure lies in its ability to harmoniously blend the old with the new, creating a unique atmosphere that captivates travelers from around the globe. The city's skyline is a testament to its modern aspirations, featuring towering skyscrapers and architectural marvels that rival those of any global metropolis. The iconic structures, such as the dazzling Burj Qatar and the futuristic Aspire Tower, symbolize Doha's ambition and desire to showcase itself as a global player on the world stage.

Yet, amidst the gleaming modernity, Doha retains its deep-rooted traditions and cultural heritage. The city proudly preserves its historic landmarks and showcases its traditions through vibrant festivals, art exhibits, and culinary experiences. Take a stroll through the bustling markets of Souq Waqif, where the aroma of spices fills the air, and vibrant textiles and traditional handicrafts line the streets. Here, you can witness the age-old traditions of falconry, indulge in authentic Qatari cuisine, and experience the warm hospitality of the locals.

As you venture further into Doha, you'll encounter a city of contrasts that continually surprises and inspires. The renowned Museum of Islamic Art, with its exquisite collection spanning centuries of artistic achievements, is a testament to the city's commitment to preserving and celebrating its cultural heritage. Meanwhile, the Katara Cultural Village provides a platform for artists and performers from around the world, showcasing the diversity of artistic expression.

Doha's love for sports and outdoor activities is evident in its state-of-the-art facilities and vast recreational spaces. From the stunning beaches along the coast to the beautifully landscaped parks, there are ample opportunities to indulge in outdoor adventures. Whether you're a fan of water sports, desert excursions, or simply relaxing in lush green oases, Doha offers a myriad of experiences to suit every taste.

The city's commitment to sustainability and environmental conservation is also noteworthy. As you explore Doha, you'll discover innovative projects that aim to protect and preserve the natural beauty of the region. The mangrove forests of Al Thakira and the stunning Inland Sea are just a glimpse of the diverse ecosystems that coexist alongside the bustling city.

In this travel guide, we invite you to delve into the essence of Doha and its surroundings, providing you with a comprehensive overview of what this remarkable city has to offer. We'll take you on a journey through its bustling markets, awe-inspiring landmarks, hidden gems, and immersive cultural experiences. Whether you're a history enthusiast, a food lover, an adventure seeker, or simply looking to indulge in luxury and relaxation, Doha promises to enchant and inspire you at every turn.

So, prepare to be captivated by the vibrant energy, the warm hospitality, and the juxtaposition of tradition and modernity that define Doha. This is a city that invites you to explore, discover, and create memories that will last a lifetime. Welcome to the enchanting world of Doha, where Arabian traditions blend seamlessly with the luxuries of a modern metropolis.

Brief History: From Bedouin Settlement to Modern Metropolis

The history of Doha is a testament to the resilience and adaptability of its people. Centuries ago, the nomadic Bedouin tribes sought refuge in the coastal area that would eventually become Doha. They recognized the potential of the region, with its access to the Arabian Gulf and abundant marine resources. The tribes relied on fishing and pearl diving for sustenance, establishing a modest settlement amidst the vast desert landscapes.

As Doha's strategic location became known, it grew in importance as a trading post. Merchants from neighboring regions flocked to Doha to exchange goods, creating a bustling marketplace that connected cultures and fostered economic growth. The city became a vibrant hub where traditional Arabian customs mingled with influences from distant lands.

The turning point for Doha came in the mid-20th century when vast oil reserves were discovered in Qatar. This discovery brought about a dramatic shift in the city's fortunes. Oil revenues flowed into the country, and Doha experienced an unprecedented wave of modernization and development. The once modest fishing village rapidly transformed into a thriving metropolis.

As the city's skyline began to change, architectural marvels started to rise. Today, Doha's iconic skyline is adorned with skyscrapers that symbolize Qatar's ambition and progress. These towering structures house multinational corporations, luxury hotels, and world-class amenities, attracting business travelers and tourists alike.

Despite its rapid growth, Doha has not forgotten its roots. The city has made a conscious effort to preserve its heritage and cultural identity. Carefully restored heritage sites, such as the historic Souq Waqif and Al Zubarah Archaeological Site, offer glimpses into Doha's past.

Walking through the vibrant souqs, where merchants still trade spices, textiles, and traditional handicrafts, visitors can feel the echoes of the city's history.

Doha is not just a city caught between the past and the present—it also embraces a vision for the future. It aspires to become a global business and cultural center, attracting talent and fostering innovation. This ambition is reflected in the city's modern sports arenas, cutting-edge museums, and educational institutions like Education City, which hosts branch campuses of prestigious international universities.

As you explore Doha, you will witness the harmonious coexistence of tradition and modernity. The vibrant street life, the graceful dhows sailing along the coast, and the remnants of ancient forts are constant reminders of Doha's heritage. At the same time, the city's futuristic skyline, its world-class museums like the Museum of Islamic Art, and its commitment to hosting major international events showcase its aspirations for the future.

In the pages that follow, this travel guide will be your companion as you uncover the wonders of Doha. We will lead you to the must-see attractions that highlight the city's historical and cultural significance. We will also reveal hidden gems off the beaten path, ensuring that you have a truly immersive experience. Whether you seek historical insights, culinary delights, outdoor adventures, or a taste of luxury, Doha offers a diverse range of experiences to suit every traveler's desires.

So, fasten your seatbelt, open your mind to new experiences, and prepare to be captivated by the allure of Doha. Let us embark on this journey together, as we unveil the secrets and treasures of this extraordinary Arabian Peninsula destination.

Essential Travel Information

Before embarking on your Doha adventure, it's crucial to gather essential travel information to ensure a smooth and enjoyable trip. Here are some key points to consider:

Best Time to Visit

Doha, the capital city of Qatar, is situated in the Arabian Peninsula and experiences a desert climate. The weather in Doha is characterized by hot summers and mild winters, making the choice of the best time to visit an important consideration for travelers.

The ideal time to visit Doha is during the winter months, from November to April. During this period, the temperatures are more moderate and pleasant, creating a comfortable environment for outdoor activities and exploration. The average temperature during winter ranges from 15°C (59°F) to 25°C (77°F), with relatively lower humidity compared to the summer months. The pleasant weather allows visitors to enjoy outdoor attractions, such as strolling along the picturesque Corniche, exploring the vibrant Souq Waqif, or taking part in various sports and recreational activities.

Winter is also the peak tourist season in Doha, as many international travelers flock to the city to escape the colder climates of their home countries. The city is buzzing with events, festivals, and cultural activities during this time. Visitors can experience the Qatar International Food Festival, explore the enchanting Katara Cultural Village, or attend sporting events like the Qatar ExxonMobil Open tennis tournament.

However, if you don't mind the heat and want to take advantage of fewer tourists and lower hotel rates, visiting Doha during the summer months can be an option. From May to October, Doha experiences extremely high temperatures, with averages ranging from 35°C (95°F) to 45°C (113°F). The scorching heat can be challenging for outdoor activities, but many indoor attractions, such as shopping malls, museums, and art galleries, provide air-conditioned havens for visitors to enjoy.

During the summer season, Doha witnesses a decrease in tourist numbers due to the intense heat, making it a less crowded time to explore the city. Hotels and resorts often offer discounted rates during this period, making it a more budget-friendly option for travelers. It's important to note that outdoor activities should be planned carefully to avoid heat exhaustion or sunburn. It is advisable to stay hydrated, wear loose-fitting, lightweight clothing, and seek shade during the hottest parts of the day.

Regardless of the time of year, it's crucial to be prepared for the weather conditions in Doha. The city experiences minimal rainfall throughout the year, with most precipitation occurring during the winter months. It's a good idea to pack sunscreen, hats, and sunglasses to protect yourself from the strong Arabian sun, regardless of the season. Carrying a refillable water bottle is also recommended to stay hydrated, especially during the hotter months.

Ultimately, the best time to visit Doha depends on personal preferences and priorities. If you prefer milder temperatures and want to participate in a range of outdoor activities, winter is the recommended season. On the other hand, if you can handle the heat and are looking for a more affordable and less crowded experience, visiting during the summer months may be a suitable option.

Regardless of the season you choose, Doha offers a plethora of attractions and experiences that showcase its unique blend of tradition and modernity. From exploring iconic landmarks and immersing in Qatari culture to indulging in world-class dining and entertainment, Doha has something to offer every visitor, no matter the time of year.

Visa Requirements

Visitors to Qatar typically require a visa, except for nationals of certain countries who are eligible for visa-free entry or visa-on-arrival. It's essential to check the visa requirements for your country of residence and apply in advance if necessary. The Qatar Ministry of Interior's official website provides up-to-date information on visa regulations and the application process.

Obtaining a Visa for Qatar

When planning your trip to Qatar, it's crucial to understand the visa requirements and processes. Qatar has specific visa policies in place to ensure the smooth entry of visitors while maintaining security and control. Here are some important points to consider when applying for a visa:

Visa Types

Qatar offers various types of visas based on the purpose and duration of the visit. The most common types include tourist visas, business visas, family visas, and transit visas. Each visa type has specific requirements and limitations, so it's essential to choose the one that best suits your travel needs.

Visa-Free Entry and Visa-on-Arrival

Nationals of certain countries are eligible for visa-free entry or visa-on-arrival in Qatar. This means that they can enter Qatar without obtaining a visa in advance or can obtain a visa upon arrival at the airport. The duration of stay for visa-on-arrival may vary depending on the nationality. It's important to check the list of eligible countries and the specific conditions for visa-free or visa-on-arrival entry.

Visa Application Process

For travelers who are not eligible for visa-free entry or visa-on-arrival, it's necessary to apply for a visa before arriving in Qatar. The application process usually involves submitting the required documents, such as a completed application form, a valid passport, passport-sized photographs, proof of accommodation, and a copy of the flight itinerary. Additionally, depending on the visa type, additional documents such as an invitation letter, sponsor's information, or proof of financial means may be required.

Applying in Advance

To avoid any travel disruptions or delays, it's advisable to apply for a visa well in advance of your planned travel dates. The processing time for visas may vary, and it's important to consider any potential delays that may occur. Applying early ensures that you have sufficient time to gather the required documents, submit the application, and receive the visa before your departure.

Qatar Ministry of Interior's Official Website

The Qatar Ministry of Interior's official website is the most reliable source for up-to-date and accurate information on visa regulations and the application process. The website provides comprehensive details on visa requirements, eligibility criteria, application forms, and any recent changes or updates. It's highly recommended to refer to the official website to obtain the most recent information before initiating the visa application process.

Assistance from Travel Agencies

If you find the visa application process complex or overwhelming, you may seek assistance from reputable travel agencies. These agencies are experienced in handling visa applications and can guide you through the process, ensuring that all the necessary documents are prepared correctly and submitted on time. However, it's important to choose a reputable agency to avoid any potential scams or fraudulent activities.

Visa Validity and Duration of Stay

Once your visa is approved, it's crucial to be aware of its validity and the duration of stay allowed. Visa validity refers to the period during which you can enter Qatar, while the duration of stay indicates the maximum number of days you can remain in the country. It's essential to comply with these limitations to avoid any legal issues or overstaying penalties.

Extension or Renewal of Visa

In some cases, you may need to extend or renew your visa while you are in Qatar. This can be due to unforeseen circumstances, changes in travel plans, or the need to stay longer than initially anticipated. To extend or renew your visa, you must follow the appropriate procedures outlined by the Qatar Ministry of Interior. It's crucial to address this well in advance of your visa's expiration to avoid any complications.

Visiting Qatar is an exciting experience, and understanding the visa requirements and application process is essential for a smooth and hassle-free trip. By checking the Qatar Ministry of Interior's official website, staying informed about the latest visa regulations, and applying in advance, you can ensure that you have the necessary documentation and approvals to enter and explore the beautiful country of Qatar.

Safety Tips

Doha is generally regarded as a safe city for travelers, with a low crime rate and a welcoming atmosphere. However, it is always wise to exercise caution and take necessary precautions to ensure a smooth and enjoyable trip. By following some essential safety tips, respecting local customs, and taking care of your well-being, you can enhance your experience in this vibrant Arabian destination.

Safety is a top priority when traveling, and Doha offers a relatively safe environment for visitors. The city has a well-established security infrastructure and a low crime rate compared to many other international destinations. However, it is still advisable to remain vigilant and take common-sense precautions to safeguard yourself and your belongings.

One of the key aspects of ensuring a safe experience in Doha is to respect the local customs and traditions. Qatar is an Islamic country with deep-rooted cultural values, and it is essential to be mindful of these when interacting with locals and visiting religious sites. Modesty is highly valued, particularly in public places and conservative areas. Both men and women should dress modestly, ensuring that shoulders and knees are covered. By dressing respectfully, you show respect for the local culture and help create a harmonious atmosphere.

When exploring Doha, it is crucial to stay aware of your surroundings and keep your belongings secure. Like any other bustling city, there can be pickpocketing or petty theft incidents in crowded areas. It is advisable to keep your valuables, such as passports, cash, and electronics, secure and close to your body. Opt for a cross-body bag or a money belt to deter potential thieves. Additionally, be cautious with your personal belongings when using public transportation, such as buses or the Doha Metro. Keep an eye on your bags and be aware of any suspicious activities around you.

Doha's climate is characterized by hot summers, and it is essential to stay hydrated, especially during the scorching summer months. The temperature can soar, and the sun's rays can be intense. Make sure to drink plenty of water throughout the day to prevent dehydration. It is also advisable to carry a reusable water bottle with you and refill it as needed. Additionally, apply sunscreen with a high SPF regularly to protect your skin from the strong sun. Wearing a wide-brimmed hat, sunglasses, and lightweight, breathable clothing can further help protect you from the heat.

In Doha, there are ample opportunities to enjoy outdoor activities, visit beautiful beaches, and explore the city's vibrant attractions. However, it is important to be mindful of your health and well-being. The hot climate can take a toll on your body, and heat exhaustion or heatstroke can be a risk if you are not careful. Take regular breaks in shaded areas or air-conditioned spaces to cool down and rest. If you start feeling unwell, seek medical assistance promptly.

In addition to the physical well-being, it is also crucial to prioritize your mental well-being while traveling. Traveling can sometimes be overwhelming, and it is natural to feel tired or stressed, especially if you are exploring a new and unfamiliar city. Allocate enough time for self-care and relaxation. Doha offers a range of wellness options, such as spas, meditation centers, and parks where you can unwind and rejuvenate. Practice self-care activities that help you find balance and peace during your journey.

Lastly, it is always a good idea to stay informed about any local advisories, travel alerts, or safety guidelines issued by the government or relevant authorities. Check the official websites or contact the embassy or consulate of your home country for the most up-to-date information before and during your trip. Being informed about any potential risks or changes in the local situation will allow you to make informed decisions and travel with confidence.

By following these safety tips, respecting local customs, and taking care of your well-being, you can have a memorable and worry-free experience in Doha. Embrace the city's rich cultural heritage, explore its attractions, and immerse yourself in the warmth and hospitality of the Qatari people. Enjoy your time in Doha, knowing that you have taken necessary precautions to make your journey safe and enjoyable.

Getting to Doha: Airports, Transportation, and Local Customs

Airports

Hamad International Airport (HIA) is the primary gateway to Doha, Qatar's vibrant capital city. Situated approximately 14 kilometers from the city center, this modern and well-equipped airport has gained a reputation as one of the world's leading aviation hubs. With its state-of-the-art facilities, extensive range of services, and convenient connectivity, HIA ensures a seamless travel experience for passengers arriving in or departing from Doha.

One of the notable features of Hamad International Airport is its impressive infrastructure. The airport's architectural design showcases a blend of modernity and Qatari heritage, with its iconic roof inspired by the traditional Bedouin tents known as "arish." This architectural marvel not only serves as a visual delight but also reflects the nation's commitment to innovation and cultural preservation.

Upon arrival at HIA, passengers are greeted by a spacious and well-organized terminal that caters to the needs of travelers from all corners of the globe. The airport offers a wide array of amenities, ensuring that passengers have a comfortable and enjoyable experience during their time at the airport.

For those seeking culinary delights, HIA boasts an impressive selection of dining options. From international cuisine to local delicacies, passengers can indulge in a variety of flavors to satisfy their cravings. Whether it's a quick bite or a leisurely meal, the airport's restaurants, cafes, and food courts offer something for every palate.

Shopaholics will be delighted by the extensive duty-free shopping available at HIA. The airport features a vast retail space, offering a diverse range of products, including luxury brands, electronics, fashion, perfumes, and souvenirs. Passengers can take advantage of tax-free shopping and find the perfect gifts for themselves or loved ones.

For those in need of relaxation or business services, HIA provides several lounges that offer a tranquil retreat from the bustling airport environment. These lounges provide comfortable seating, complimentary refreshments, Wi-Fi access, and other amenities, allowing passengers to unwind or catch up on work before their flights.

In addition to the wide range of amenities, HIA places a strong emphasis on passenger convenience and efficiency. The airport provides excellent connectivity with numerous international airlines operating flights to and from Doha. Whether you're flying from major cities in Europe, Asia, the Americas, or elsewhere, HIA offers excellent accessibility, making it a preferred choice for travelers worldwide.

The airport's state-of-the-art facilities include efficient check-in counters, automated immigration systems, and streamlined security procedures, ensuring that passengers can move through the airport smoothly. The well-trained and friendly staff are dedicated to providing exceptional service, further enhancing the overall travel experience.

HIA's commitment to sustainability is also worth noting. As an environmentally conscious airport, HIA has implemented several initiatives to reduce its carbon footprint and promote sustainable practices. These include energy-efficient lighting, waste management systems, and the use of eco-friendly materials in construction. The airport's focus on sustainability aligns with Qatar's broader vision of environmental stewardship and contributes to a greener future.

Hamad International Airport not only serves as a gateway to Doha but also offers a glimpse into Qatar's culture and hospitality. From the moment passengers arrive, they are immersed in the country's warm and welcoming atmosphere, setting the tone for their exploration of Qatar's rich heritage and modern attractions.

For those with a layover or extended waiting time, HIA provides opportunities for a brief taste of Qatari culture. The airport features art installations, exhibitions, and cultural displays that showcase the nation's artistic and historical treasures. Passengers can admire the works of renowned local and international artists, gaining a deeper appreciation for Qatar's vibrant arts scene.

Overall, Hamad International Airport stands as a testament to Qatar's commitment to excellence and innovation. Its world-class facilities, extensive amenities, and convenient connectivity make it an integral part of the travel experience for visitors to Doha. Whether you're arriving for business or leisure, HIA sets the stage for a memorable journey, reflecting Qatar's vision of becoming a global destination of choice.

As passengers bid farewell to Hamad International Airport, they leave with a lasting impression of a city that seamlessly blends tradition and modernity, offering a captivating glimpse into the wonders of Doha and the Arabian Peninsula.

Transportation

Public transportation in Doha is well-developed and offers a reliable way to navigate the city and explore its attractions. With options including buses, the Doha Metro, taxis, and even rental cars, travelers have various choices to suit their preferences and needs.

The Doha Metro, in particular, has become a popular and convenient mode of transportation within the city. It consists of three lines: the Red Line, Green Line, and Gold Line, which connect key areas and attractions. Each line is color-coded, making it easy for travelers to identify the correct route. The metro system operates from around 6:00 a.m. to 11:00 p.m. on weekdays, with extended hours on weekends.

The Red Line, the longest line of the Doha Metro, runs from Al Wakra in the south to Lusail in the north, passing through major areas such as Hamad International Airport, West Bay, and Education City. This line is particularly convenient for visitors arriving at the airport, as it provides a direct connection to the city center and various hotels.

The Green Line, on the other hand, connects Al Riffa in the east to Al Mansoura in the west. This line serves popular destinations such as Souq Waqif, Aspire Park, and Qatar National Library. It provides easy access to cultural and recreational attractions, as well as residential areas.

The Gold Line, although shorter in length, serves as an important connection between the Red Line and the Green Line. It runs from Ras Bu Abboud in the east to Al Aziziyah in the west, passing through Education City and Al Rayyan Stadium. The Gold Line is particularly useful for travelers who want to explore the Education City complex, which houses several universities, research institutions, and cultural facilities.

The Doha Metro offers a convenient and efficient way to travel, with air-conditioned stations and trains, frequent service, and clear signage in both Arabic and English. The ticketing system is straightforward, with reusable travel cards that can be purchased at the stations or vending machines. These cards can be loaded with credit and used for multiple journeys, providing a cost-effective option for frequent travelers.

In addition to the metro, buses in Doha provide an extensive network that covers various areas of the city. Mowasalat, the state-owned transportation company, operates the bus services, and the routes are well-planned, serving residential areas, commercial districts, and popular landmarks. Buses are a more affordable option compared to taxis, and they offer a chance to experience the city from a different perspective. The bus stops are clearly marked, and schedules can be obtained from the Mowasalat website or at the bus stations.

For those who prefer the convenience and flexibility of private transportation, **taxis** are widely available in Doha. Taxis can be hailed on the street, found at designated taxi stands, or booked through mobile applications such as Karwa and Uber. The drivers are generally reliable and knowledgeable about the city, making it easy to reach specific destinations. It's advisable to ensure the taxi meter is used or agree on a fare before starting the journey.

Another option for travelers in Doha is renting a car. **Renting a car** in Doha is an excellent option for travelers seeking the ultimate flexibility and independence during their visit. Several reputable rental car companies operate in the city, offering a wide selection of vehicles to cater to different budgets and preferences. Renting a car provides the freedom to explore Doha at your own pace and venture beyond the city limits to discover the captivating sights and landscapes of Qatar.

Before embarking on a self-driving adventure in Doha, there are a few important factors to consider. Firstly, it's crucial to familiarize yourself with the traffic regulations and rules of the road in Qatar. Like many other countries, Doha follows right-hand traffic, meaning vehicles drive on the right side of the road. It's essential to adhere to speed limits, traffic signs, and signals to ensure a safe and enjoyable driving experience.

To rent a car in Doha, you will need a valid driver's license. If you have an international driving permit (IDP), it is highly recommended to carry it along with your original driver's license from your home country. The IDP serves as a recognized translation of your license and can provide additional verification to local authorities if necessary. However, it's important to note that regulations may vary, so it's advisable to check the specific requirements with the rental car company or the Qatar Traffic Department.

When renting a car, it's essential to consider your budget, preferences, and the nature of your planned activities. Rental car companies in Doha offer a range of vehicles, from economy cars to luxury sedans and SUVs, allowing you to choose the one that suits your needs and style. It's advisable to book your rental car in advance, especially during peak travel seasons, to ensure availability and secure the best rates.

One of the advantages of renting a car in Doha is the convenience of exploring the city's diverse neighborhoods and attractions. From the bustling streets of Souq Waqif to the modern skyscrapers of West Bay, having a car allows you to navigate between different areas effortlessly. Moreover, if you plan to visit attractions outside of Doha, such as the mesmerizing sand dunes of the Qatari desert or the historical sites in the coastal town of Al Zubarah, a rental car gives you the freedom to reach these destinations with ease.

When driving in Doha, it's important to keep in mind the availability and cost of parking facilities. While many hotels, shopping malls, and attractions offer designated parking areas, it's advisable to check the parking options and any associated fees in advance. Be mindful of parking regulations and avoid parking in restricted areas or blocking traffic. It's recommended to lock your car and avoid leaving valuables in plain sight to ensure the security of your belongings.

Before setting off on your self-driving adventure, it can be helpful to plan your routes using navigation applications or maps. Familiarize yourself with the major roads, highways, and landmarks to ensure a smooth and efficient journey. Qatar's infrastructure is well-developed, with well-maintained roads and clear signage in both Arabic and English, making it relatively easy to navigate around the city.

In case of emergencies or unexpected incidents on the road, it's advisable to have contact information for the rental car company readily available. They can provide assistance, guidance, or arrange for a replacement vehicle if needed. Additionally, it's recommended to have a mobile phone with a reliable network connection to stay connected and access any necessary information during your travels.

When utilizing public transportation in Doha, it's helpful to keep in mind a few practical tips. Firstly, it's advisable to carry a map or use navigation applications to familiarize yourself with the routes and destinations. The Doha Metro app, for example, provides real-time information on train timings, station locations, and fares. Secondly, it's important to plan your journey in advance, considering factors such as peak hours and potential transfers between lines or modes of transportation. Thirdly, be prepared for crowded conditions during rush hours, particularly on the metro and buses. Lastly, respect the designated seating areas and priority seating for elderly individuals, pregnant women, and people with disabilities.

Overall, Doha's well-developed public transportation system, including the Doha Metro, buses, taxis, and rental cars, offers travelers a range of options to explore the city and its surrounding areas. Whether you prefer the convenience of the metro, the affordability of buses, the flexibility of taxis, or the freedom of a rental car, there is a mode of transportation that suits your needs. Embrace the convenience and efficiency of public transportation in Doha as you navigate the city's vibrant neighborhoods, immerse yourself in its cultural heritage, and discover its modern marvels.

Local Customs

Qatar is an Islamic country, and visitors should respect local customs and traditions.

Dress Modestly, especially in Public Places and Religious Sites. Both Men and Women should cover their Shoulders and Knees.

When visiting Doha, it is important to be mindful of the local culture and dress modestly, especially in public places and religious sites. Qatar is an Islamic country with strong cultural values, and respecting the local customs regarding attire demonstrates cultural sensitivity and helps visitors integrate better with the local community. Here are some guidelines to follow regarding dress code in Doha:

Women's Attire

- Women are expected to dress modestly, covering their shoulders and knees in public.
- It is advisable to wear loose-fitting clothing that covers the arms and legs, such as long-sleeved tops, tunics, or maxi dresses.
- Avoid clothing that is tight, revealing, or transparent, as it may be considered inappropriate.
- Wearing a headscarf is not mandatory for non-Muslim women, but it is respectful to carry a scarf to cover the head when entering religious sites.

Men's Attire

- Men are also expected to dress modestly, particularly in public places and religious sites.
- It is recommended to wear shirts with sleeves and long trousers or knee-length shorts.
- Avoid wearing sleeveless shirts, tank tops, or clothing with offensive slogans or images.

Public Displays of Affection should be Avoided, as they are Considered Inappropriate.

In Doha, public displays of affection, such as kissing, hugging, or holding hands, are considered inappropriate and are not culturally accepted. Qatar is a conservative society with strong Islamic values, and public intimacy is generally not encouraged. To ensure a comfortable and respectful experience in Doha, it is advisable to keep affectionate gestures private and express them in more appropriate settings. It is important to note that while locals understand that visitors may have different cultural norms, respecting their customs fosters positive interactions and promotes cultural understanding.

Alcohol Consumption is Allowed in Designated Areas such as Hotels and Licensed Establishments but is Strictly Prohibited in Public Places.

Qatar follows strict regulations regarding the consumption of alcohol due to its adherence to Islamic law. While alcohol is permitted in designated areas, such as hotels and licensed establishments, it is strictly prohibited in public places. Here's what you need to know about alcohol consumption in Doha:

Hotels: Most hotels in Doha have bars and restaurants that serve alcoholic beverages to guests. These establishments are licensed and provide a range of alcoholic options. Visitors staying at hotels with alcohol service can enjoy their drinks within the premises of the hotel without any issues.

Licensed Establishments: There are a limited number of licensed restaurants, bars, and clubs outside of hotels that are authorized to serve alcohol. These establishments have obtained special permits and licenses to offer alcoholic beverages to customers. They provide a vibrant nightlife scene for those seeking entertainment and socializing opportunities.

Public Places: It is essential to note that consuming alcohol in public places, including parks, streets, and beaches, is strictly prohibited. Qatar has implemented strict laws to maintain public order and ensure that cultural sensitivities are respected. Violating these regulations can lead to legal consequences.

When visiting Doha, it is advisable to familiarize yourself with the specific rules and regulations regarding alcohol consumption. It is also important to respect local customs and avoid excessive or disruptive behavior while consuming alcohol in designated areas. This will help you enjoy your experience in Doha while ensuring that you comply with local laws and cultural norms.

Useful Apps And Websites For Travelers

Visit Qatar (App): The Visit Qatar app serves as the ultimate companion for travelers exploring Doha. This official tourism app provides a wealth of comprehensive information about the city's attractions, events, restaurants, hotels, and transportation options. With a user-friendly interface and intuitive navigation, the app ensures that you have all the essential information at your fingertips.

Upon opening the Visit Qatar app, you'll find a vast array of attractions and landmarks to discover. From iconic skyscrapers to cultural sites, the app offers detailed descriptions, stunning photos, and essential visitor information for each location. Whether you're interested in exploring the magnificent Museum of Islamic Art, strolling along the waterfront at the Corniche, or venturing into the vibrant Souq Waqif, the app provides insightful information to help you plan your visit.

To assist with itinerary planning, the Visit Qatar app offers suggested itineraries based on different interests and timeframes. Whether you have a few hours or several days in Doha, you can find pre-designed itineraries that cover the city's highlights and hidden gems. These itineraries include suggested routes, attractions, and dining options, ensuring you make the most of your time in Doha.

One of the standout features of the Visit Qatar app is its interactive maps. These maps allow you to navigate the city easily, locate attractions, and find nearby amenities. You can customize the map view based on your preferences, whether you're looking for restaurants, hotels, shopping centers, or transportation options. With GPS functionality, the app also provides real-time directions, ensuring you never get lost while exploring Doha.

For those seeking exclusive deals and discounts, the Visit Qatar app offers a section dedicated to special offers and promotions. You can find discounts on hotel bookings, attractions, tours, and more, allowing you to save money while enjoying the best that Doha has to offer.

Talabat (App/Website): Talabat is a must-have app for food enthusiasts visiting Doha. Whether you're craving local Qatari cuisine or international flavors, Talabat offers a convenient and hassle-free way to browse and order from a wide range of restaurants in the city. With a simple and user-friendly interface, the app allows you to explore menus, read reviews, and place orders for delivery or pickup.

Talabat's extensive restaurant selection includes options for every taste and budget. From fine dining establishments to casual eateries and popular fast-food chains, you can discover a diverse range of culinary experiences through the app. Whether you're in the mood for traditional Arabic dishes like biryani or kebabs, or you prefer international cuisine such as sushi or pizza, Talabat ensures that your food cravings are satisfied.

One of the key advantages of Talabat is its convenience. After selecting your desired restaurant and dishes, you can customize your order, specify delivery or pickup preferences, and proceed with secure online payment. The app provides real-time updates on the status of your order, allowing you to track its progress and estimated delivery time.

Karwa (App): Getting around Doha is made easy with the Karwa app, the official transportation app of the city. Whether you need a taxi, a limousine, or information about public buses, Karwa offers a convenient and reliable way to navigate the city's transportation options.

With the Karwa app, you can book a taxi or a limousine directly from your smartphone. The app provides real-time tracking of the assigned vehicle, allowing you to monitor its location and estimated arrival time. You can also choose from various payment options, including cash or card, making your journey hassle-free.

In addition to booking taxis and limousines, the Karwa app provides information about Doha's public bus system. You can access bus routes, schedules, and fares, helping you plan your journeys and navigate the city's extensive network of bus routes. The app also includes a journey planner feature, which suggests the most convenient bus routes based on your starting point and destination.

Qatar Events (Website): To stay updated with the vibrant cultural scene in Doha, Qatar Events is an indispensable website. With a comprehensive listing of upcoming events, concerts, exhibitions, festivals, and cultural performances, this website ensures that you don't miss out on any exciting experiences during your visit.

If you're interested in attending a musical concert, exploring an art exhibition, or participating in a local festival, Qatar Events provides detailed information about each event. You can find dates, timings, venues, ticket prices, and descriptions, allowing you to plan your itinerary accordingly. The website also allows you to filter events based on categories such as music, art, sports, and family-friendly activities, making it easier to find events that align with your interests.

By regularly checking Qatar Events, you can discover both well-known and hidden gems within Doha's vibrant cultural calendar. From traditional Qatari performances to international artists and world-class exhibitions, the website offers a diverse range of cultural experiences that cater to all tastes.

Zomato (App/Website): Zomato is a popular app and website for food enthusiasts looking to explore the diverse culinary scene in Doha. Whether you're searching for a specific cuisine, seeking recommendations, or looking for a particular dining ambiance, Zomato provides a comprehensive platform to discover and explore restaurants in the city.

Upon opening the Zomato app or website, you can search for restaurants based on various filters such as cuisine, location, price range, and user ratings. Each restaurant listing includes detailed information, menus, photos, and user reviews, allowing you to make informed dining choices. Whether you're looking for a romantic fine-dining experience, a casual café, or a family-friendly restaurant, Zomato helps you find the perfect spot.

One of the key features of Zomato is its extensive user-generated content. Users can rate and review restaurants, providing insights and personal experiences that aid in decision-making. You can browse through authentic reviews, check ratings, and read comments to get a sense of the overall dining experience at a particular restaurant.

Zomato also goes beyond just restaurant listings. It provides additional features such as online table reservations, food delivery options, and menus with prices.

Qatar Airways (App): If you're flying with Qatar Airways or planning to book flights to and from Doha, the Qatar Airways app is an essential tool that ensures a seamless travel experience. From managing your bookings to accessing exclusive offers and staying updated on flight statuses, the app provides a range of features to enhance your journey.

With the Qatar Airways app, you can conveniently manage your flight bookings, check-in online, and access your boarding pass directly from your smartphone. The app also provides real-time flight status updates, including gate changes, departure times, and baggage claim information, ensuring that you stay informed throughout your journey.

For those looking for exclusive offers and discounts, the Qatar Airways app provides access to special promotions and deals. Whether it's discounted fares, additional baggage allowance, or access to airport lounges, the app ensures that you're aware of the latest offers and can take advantage of them when planning your travel.

Additionally, the app offers a range of services and features to make your travel experience more convenient. You can track your Privilege Club loyalty program status, access in-flight entertainment options, and explore destination guides for Qatar Airways' extensive network of destinations.

Doha Bus (Website): Doha Bus offers hop-on-hop-off sightseeing tours that cover major attractions in Doha, allowing you to explore the city at your own pace. Their website serves as a valuable resource for information about routes, schedules, and ticket options, making it easier for you to plan your sightseeing adventures.

By visiting the Doha Bus website, you can access detailed information about the different tour routes available. Each route covers a specific set of attractions and landmarks, and the website provides descriptions and photos of each stop, allowing you to decide which ones you'd like to explore further. Whether you're interested in the modern architecture of the West Bay area or the cultural heritage of Souq Waqif, the website helps you choose the most suitable route.

The website also provides schedules for each route, including the frequency of buses and operating hours.

This allows you to plan your day effectively and ensure that you don't miss out on any attractions. Additionally, the website offers information about ticket options, including single-day passes and multi-day passes, allowing you to choose the best option for your sightseeing needs.

MoI Qatar (App): The MoI Qatar app, developed by the Ministry of Interior, provides essential services for residents and visitors in Qatar. While primarily designed for residents, the app offers features that can be useful for visitors as well.

One of the key features of the MoI Qatar app is the ability to check visa status. If you're visiting Qatar and require a visa, the app allows you to track the progress of your visa application and check the current status. This feature provides peace of mind and ensures that you stay updated on your visa processing.

The app also offers e-services that can be useful for visitors. These e-services include the ability to apply for permits, such as driving licenses or residence permits, if you're staying in Qatar for an extended period. While these services may not be applicable to all visitors, they can be valuable for those planning to work, study, or reside in Qatar for an extended period.

Additionally, the MoI Qatar app provides important updates related to safety and security in Qatar. This includes notifications about any emergencies, alerts, or advisories that may affect visitors. By staying connected to the app, you can receive timely information and ensure that you stay informed during your time in Qatar.

Qatar Living (Website): Qatar Living is a popular online community platform that offers a wealth of information about living, working, and exploring Qatar. While primarily designed for residents, the website serves as a valuable resource for visitors to Doha as well.

By visiting the Qatar Living website, you can access a wide range of information and resources that can enhance your visit to Doha. The website features classifieds, allowing you to browse listings for accommodation, vehicles, and various services. This can be particularly useful if you're looking for short-term rentals, transportation options, or other amenities during your stay.

The Qatar Living forums provide a platform for discussions and interactions among residents and visitors. By browsing through the forums, you can find tips, recommendations, and answers to common questions about living and exploring Doha. Whether you're seeking advice on the best places to eat, recommendations for attractions, or insights into the local culture, the forums can provide valuable information.

Additionally, Qatar Living features a news section that covers various topics and current affairs in Qatar. By staying updated with the latest news and events, you can gain a deeper understanding of the country and its culture. The website also offers guides and articles that provide insights into various aspects of living in Qatar, including travel tips, cultural etiquette, and local customs.

The Entertainer (App): The Entertainer is a digital app that offers exclusive discounts and buy-one-get-one-free deals for various attractions, restaurants, spas, and activities in Doha. By downloading the app and purchasing a subscription, you can access a wide range of offers that allow you to save money and make the most of your experiences in the city.

The Entertainer app provides a vast selection of deals and discounts for popular venues and activities in Doha. Whether you're looking to dine at a high-end restaurant, enjoy a spa treatment, or explore local attractions, the app offers significant savings. The buy-one-get-one-free feature allows you to enjoy two-for-one deals, essentially doubling the value of your experiences.

The app provides a user-friendly interface that allows you to search for deals based on categories, locations, and specific venues. You can also browse through curated collections and recommendations to discover new experiences. The app provides detailed information about each offer, including terms and conditions, allowing you to make informed choices.

By using The Entertainer app, you can enjoy significant savings on your dining, entertainment, and leisure activities, making your visit to Doha more affordable and enjoyable.

Uber (App): Uber is a widely used ride-hailing app in Doha, providing convenient transportation options at competitive prices. By downloading the Uber app and creating an account, you can easily request a car and navigate the city without the need for cash transactions.

Using the Uber app, you can enter your pick-up and drop-off locations, and the app will connect you with available drivers in your area. You can track the driver's location in real-time, receive estimated arrival times, and even communicate with the driver if needed.

Uber offers different types of services in Doha, including UberX, UberSELECT, and UberXL, allowing you to choose the most suitable option based on your preferences and group size. The app provides transparent pricing, and you can see the fare estimate before confirming your ride.

One of the advantages of using Uber is the cashless payment system. Payment is made through the app using your registered credit or debit card, eliminating the need for cash transactions or dealing with local currencies.

Doha Metro (App): The Doha Metro app is essential for utilizing the city's efficient and modern metro system.

The app provides information about routes, timetables, station locations, and fare options, making it easier to travel around Doha using public transportation.

With the Doha Metro app, you can plan your journeys by accessing the metro map and finding the nearest stations to your starting point and destination. The app provides details about each station, including facilities, connecting bus routes, and nearby attractions. You can also view the timetable for each line, ensuring that you're aware of the frequency of trains and their operating hours.

The app offers fare information and options for purchasing tickets. You can choose between single-trip tickets or reusable travel cards, depending on your travel needs. The app also includes a journey planner feature, allowing you to input your starting point and destination to receive suggested routes and connections.

Google Maps: in Doha is a reliable and widely used navigation tool that provides detailed maps, directions, and real-time traffic information. If you're exploring the city or navigating through the streets of Doha, Google Maps can assist you in finding your way to various attractions, restaurants, hotels, and other points of interest.

Where To Get Physical Maps Of Doha
Visit the local visitor information centers, such as the Qatar Tourism Authority (QTA) Visitor Information Center or the Hamad International Airport Information

Desk. These centers often provide free maps and brochures to assist tourists.

Hotels and Accommodations: Many hotels in Doha offer physical maps to their guests upon check-in. You can inquire at the front desk or concierge of your hotel to see if they have maps available.

These apps and websites will assist you in navigating, exploring, and enjoying your visit to Doha by providing valuable information, services, and convenient solutions to enhance your travel experience.

CHAPTER TWO

EXPLORING DOHA'S ICONIC LANDMARKS

Doha, the vibrant capital of Qatar, is home to a myriad of iconic landmarks that beautifully blend tradition and modernity. Embark on a captivating journey through the city and immerse yourself in its rich cultural tapestry. Here are some of Doha's must-visit landmarks:

The Pearl-Qatar: Luxury, Art, and Entertainment on an Island

Situated on an artificial island, The Pearl-Qatar is a luxurious waterfront development that epitomizes elegance and grandeur. This stunning destination in Doha invites visitors to immerse themselves in a world of luxury, art, and entertainment. As you step onto the marina promenade, you'll be greeted by a mesmerizing blend of architectural marvels, extravagant yachts, and a vibrant atmosphere that exudes sophistication.

The Pearl-Qatar's marina promenade is a haven for fashion enthusiasts and avid shoppers. Lined with high-end boutiques and designer stores, it offers a premier shopping experience. Fashionistas can browse through a range of renowned international brands, from haute couture to luxury accessories. Discover the latest trends, indulge in some retail therapy, and find exquisite pieces to enhance your wardrobe.

After satisfying your shopping cravings, allow yourself to be transported into a culinary paradise. The Pearl-Qatar boasts a remarkable selection of dining establishments that cater to all tastes and preferences. From world-class fine dining restaurants helmed by renowned chefs to trendy cafes and bistros, the options are endless. Sample delectable cuisines from around the globe, including Mediterranean, Asian fusion, Middle Eastern, and more. Indulge in gastronomic delights that showcase the finest ingredients and innovative culinary techniques, ensuring a memorable dining experience.

While exploring The Pearl-Qatar, take a moment to appreciate the captivating art installations that adorn the surroundings. The island's public spaces and walkways serve as a canvas for contemporary art, making it a dynamic and visually stimulating environment. From sculptures and interactive installations to vibrant murals, the artistic elements add an extra layer of charm and creativity to the luxurious ambiance. Allow yourself to be captivated by the unique blend of art and architecture, creating an immersive experience that is truly unforgettable.

As you continue your journey through The Pearl-Qatar, be sure to take in the picturesque views of the Arabian Gulf. The island's waterfront location offers breathtaking panoramas of the azure waters, dotted with magnificent yachts and sailboats. Find a comfortable spot along the promenade, bask in the gentle sea breeze, and admire the beauty of the surroundings. The tranquil ambiance provides a serene escape from the bustling city, allowing you to unwind and rejuvenate.

In addition to its shopping, dining, and artistic offerings, The Pearl-Qatar hosts a variety of events and entertainment options throughout the year. From live performances and concerts to art exhibitions and cultural festivals, there's always something happening on the island. Immerse yourself in the vibrant social scene, mingle with like-minded individuals, and embrace the lively energy that fills the air.

The Pearl-Qatar is not just a destination for visitors but also an exclusive residential community. Its exquisite residential towers and villas offer a luxurious lifestyle with stunning views and world-class amenities. Whether you choose to stay in one of the waterfront apartments or elegant villas, you'll have access to a range of facilities, including private beach clubs, fitness centers, and swimming pools. Residents can also enjoy a sense of community through social events and gatherings organized within the neighborhood.

Overall, The Pearl-Qatar is a destination that seamlessly blends luxury, art, and entertainment, creating an unparalleled experience for visitors and residents alike. It is a testament to Qatar's commitment to creating a cosmopolitan hub that embraces sophistication and innovation. Whether you're seeking a memorable shopping spree, a gourmet culinary adventure, or simply a serene waterfront escape, The Pearl-Qatar offers an enchanting setting that will exceed your expectations. Immerse yourself in this world of elegance and indulge in the pleasures that await you on this captivating artificial island in Doha.

Souq Waqif: A Traditional Market Bursting with Authentic Flavors

Step back in time and immerse yourself in the vibrant ambiance of Souq Waqif, a bustling traditional market that stands as a testament to Qatar's rich heritage. As you enter this captivating marketplace, you are immediately transported to a bygone era, where the sights, sounds, and scents create an enchanting atmosphere.

The moment you step foot into Souq Waqif, you'll find yourself surrounded by a labyrinth of narrow alleys, each one beckoning you to explore further. The market is a treasure trove of authentic Qatari culture, with shops and stalls brimming with an array of colorful textiles, spices, perfumes, and handicrafts. The vibrant tapestry of colors and textures will undoubtedly captivate your senses and ignite your curiosity.

As you wander through the bustling lanes, you'll encounter friendly vendors eager to showcase their wares and share their stories. Haggle with them as you peruse the intricately woven rugs, embroidered fabrics, and

Bedouin jewelry. The art of negotiation is an integral part of the Souq Waqif experience, and engaging in friendly banter with the vendors can often lead to delightful surprises and fair deals.

One of the highlights of Souq Waqif is undoubtedly the tantalizing array of local delicacies available at the numerous restaurants and cafes scattered throughout the market. Indulge in the flavors of Qatari cuisine as you savor dishes like machbous (spiced rice with meat), harees (meat and wheat porridge), and luqaimat (sweet dumplings). Whether you choose to dine in one of the traditional courtyard-style restaurants or opt for a more casual street food experience, each bite will transport you deeper into the heart of Qatari gastronomy.

As you navigate through Souq Waqif, be prepared to encounter a myriad of sights and experiences. Take a moment to appreciate the architectural beauty of the restored buildings, showcasing traditional Qatari designs with their wooden balconies and ornate facades. The attention to detail in preserving the market's historical authenticity is evident in every nook and cranny.

Throughout the day, the market comes alive with a diverse range of activities and entertainment. Street performers, musicians, and local artisans contribute to the lively atmosphere, adding a touch of cultural vibrancy to your visit. Traditional music performances and folk dances often grace the courtyards, providing a glimpse into the rich artistic heritage of Qatar.

Souq Waqif is not just a place for shopping and dining; it is also a cultural hub where you can immerse yourself in Qatari traditions. Visit the Falcon Souq to witness the time-honored tradition of falconry, an integral part of Qatari heritage. Admire the majestic birds and learn about their significance in the local culture.

For a more serene experience, head to the spice market and breathe in the aromatic scents of exotic spices such as saffron, cardamom, and cinnamon. Let the fragrances guide you through the stalls as you explore the diverse array of herbs, dried fruits, and incense.

To delve even deeper into Qatari culture, visit the Souq Waqif Art Center, where local artists showcase their talent through traditional and contemporary art forms. Admire the intricate calligraphy, vibrant paintings, and stunning sculptures that offer a glimpse into the creative spirit of Qatar.

As the day transitions into evening, Souq Waqif takes on a magical allure. The market is beautifully illuminated, casting a warm glow on the bustling crowds. This is the perfect time to unwind at one of the rooftop terraces or outdoor cafes, where you can sip on a cup of traditional Qatari coffee, fragrant with cardamom, and revel in the ambiance of this captivating place.

Souq Waqif is more than just a market; it is a living testament to the resilience of Qatari culture and a haven for locals and visitors alike to connect with the past while embracing the present. It serves as a vibrant center where traditions are upheld, stories are shared, and the essence of Qatar's heritage is preserved.

A visit to Souq Waqif is an immersive experience that transports you to a different time and place. Lose yourself in the labyrinthine alleys, haggle with friendly vendors, and soak up the lively atmosphere that reverberates with the spirit of Qatar. This bustling traditional market is not just a place to shop and dine; it's a journey into the heart and soul of Qatari culture, a sensory delight that will leave an indelible mark on your travel memories.

Katara Cultural Village: Showcasing Qatar's Artistic and Cultural Heritage

Nestled along the sparkling shores of Doha, Katara Cultural Village stands as a testament to Qatar's commitment to promoting its artistic and cultural legacy. This vibrant hub offers visitors a captivating journey through a myriad of activities that encompass various forms of artistic expression. From art exhibitions and theatrical performances to music concerts and film screenings, Katara Cultural Village is a haven for those seeking to immerse themselves in Qatar's rich heritage and creative spirit.

As you step into Katara Cultural Village, you are greeted by a mesmerizing blend of traditional Qatari architecture and contemporary design. The meticulously crafted buildings and open-air spaces reflect the nation's deep-rooted appreciation for its cultural heritage while embracing modern aesthetics. Every corner of the village exudes an air of creativity, inviting visitors to explore and discover the treasures it holds.

One of the highlights of Katara Cultural Village is its beautifully designed amphitheater, a striking venue that hosts a myriad of performances and cultural events. With a seating capacity of thousands, this open-air theater serves as a stage for world-class musical concerts, captivating theatrical productions, and mesmerizing dance performances. From classical music to traditional Qatari performances, the amphitheater showcases a diverse array of talents, fostering cross-cultural exchange and artistic appreciation.

Venturing further into the village, you will encounter a wealth of art galleries that showcase both local and international works. These galleries provide a platform for artists to display their creations and engage with visitors on a deeper level. Each exhibition is carefully curated, offering a diverse range of artistic styles and themes that reflect the multifaceted nature of Qatar's contemporary art scene. From paintings and sculptures to multimedia installations, the galleries at Katara Cultural Village serve as a window into the ever-evolving world of visual arts.

In addition to the galleries, Katara Cultural Village also offers a multitude of workshops and educational programs designed to engage visitors of all ages. These workshops provide a unique opportunity to learn traditional Qatari crafts, such as calligraphy, pottery, and weaving, under the guidance of skilled artisans. Through hands-on experiences, participants can gain a deeper understanding of the rich cultural heritage that has shaped Qatar's identity. The workshops not only foster a sense of appreciation for traditional arts and crafts but also encourage the preservation of these time-honored traditions for future generations.

Katara Cultural Village is also renowned for its annual festivals that celebrate a diverse range of cultural traditions from around the world. These vibrant festivals bring together artists, musicians, performers, and visitors from different backgrounds to engage in a global cultural exchange. From the Qatar International Food Festival to the Doha Jazz Festival, these events showcase the vibrancy and diversity of Qatar's cultural scene, creating an atmosphere of celebration and unity.

For film enthusiasts, Katara Cultural Village is home to the Katara Cinema, a state-of-the-art theater that screens an eclectic selection of films from both local and international filmmakers. The cinema hosts regular screenings, film festivals, and discussions, providing a platform for dialogue and exploration of various cinematic works. Whether it's classic films, contemporary documentaries, or thought-provoking independent movies, the Katara Cinema offers a unique cinematic experience that caters to all tastes.

Apart from its artistic and cultural offerings, Katara Cultural Village is also home to a variety of dining options that showcase the flavors of Qatar and the wider Arab region. From traditional Qatari cuisine to international fare, the restaurants and cafes within the village provide a culinary journey that tantalizes the taste buds. Visitors can savor aromatic Arabic coffee, indulge in delectable Middle Eastern sweets, or enjoy a sumptuous feast of traditional Qatari dishes.

As the day draws to a close, the village comes alive with enchanting nighttime performances that illuminate the surroundings. The lights dance across the intricate architectural details, creating a magical ambiance that heightens the sensory experience. The serene beauty of the village under the moonlight provides a serene backdrop for contemplation and reflection.

Katara Cultural Village is not just a place to visit; it is an immersive experience that transports visitors into the heart and soul of Qatar's artistic and cultural tapestry. By promoting artistic expression, fostering cross-cultural dialogue, and preserving traditional heritage, Katara Cultural Village plays a vital role in shaping Qatar's identity as a global hub of creativity and cultural exchange.

Museum of Islamic Art: A Magnificent Collection of Islamic Artifacts

Perched gracefully on the Corniche waterfront, the Museum of Islamic Art in Doha stands as a testament to Qatar's deep respect and admiration for Islamic art and heritage. Designed by the legendary architect I.M. Pei, this architectural masterpiece is not only a visual delight but also a treasure trove of Islamic artifacts that spans over 1,400 years of history. As you step into this cultural haven, you will be captivated by the meticulously curated collection that showcases the richness, diversity, and artistic brilliance of Islamic culture.

The Museum of Islamic Art is a soaring symbol of Qatar's commitment to preserving and celebrating its cultural heritage. Its striking geometric façade and clean lines pay homage to Islamic architectural traditions while exuding a sense of modernity. The building's design incorporates elements inspired by ancient Islamic forts, evoking a sense of grandeur and reverence as you approach its entrance.

Upon entering the museum, you are greeted by a spacious atrium flooded with natural light, enhancing the serene ambiance. The interior spaces are thoughtfully designed to create an immersive experience, allowing visitors to delve into the captivating world of Islamic art. The galleries are organized chronologically, guiding you through different periods and regions, offering a comprehensive overview of the artistic evolution within the Islamic world.

One of the highlights of the museum is its extensive collection of Islamic artifacts. From delicate calligraphy to exquisite ceramics, from vibrant textiles to rare manuscripts, each piece exemplifies the mastery and skill of Islamic artisans throughout the centuries. The museum's collection includes works from various Islamic dynasties and regions, including the Arab world, Persia, India, and Andalusia.

As you wander through the galleries, you will encounter masterpieces that leave you in awe. The intricately illuminated Qur'ans, adorned with gold leaf and vibrant pigments, display the sacredness and beauty of Islamic calligraphy. These ancient manuscripts not only serve as religious texts but also showcase the extraordinary craftsmanship and devotion of the scribes who painstakingly transcribed the sacred verses.

Ceramics hold a prominent place in Islamic art, and the museum's collection boasts a remarkable array of pottery and tiles. From the dazzling blue and white patterns of Chinese-inspired ceramics to the vibrant floral motifs of Persian and Iznik tiles, the variety and intricacy of the designs are a testament to the cross-cultural exchange that shaped Islamic artistic traditions.

The museum also showcases a stunning collection of textiles, including intricately woven carpets, luxurious textiles, and embroidered garments. These textiles exemplify the mastery of techniques such as silk weaving, tapestry, and intricate embroidery. Each piece tells a story of the cultural and historical context in which it was created, reflecting the diverse influences that shaped Islamic textile traditions.

Beyond the permanent collection, the Museum of Islamic Art frequently hosts temporary exhibitions that delve deeper into specific themes, artists, or historical periods. These exhibitions offer a fresh perspective and provide a platform to showcase lesser-known facets of Islamic art, introducing visitors to new narratives and expanding their understanding of this rich artistic tradition.

In addition to the captivating exhibits, the museum offers various educational programs, workshops, and lectures, catering to visitors of all ages and interests. These initiatives aim to foster a deeper appreciation and understanding of Islamic art and its significance in shaping world culture. Whether you are a seasoned art enthusiast or a curious learner, the museum provides ample opportunities to engage with the collection and explore the nuances of Islamic art through guided tours or self-guided exploration.

To enhance the overall experience, the Museum of Islamic Art houses a stunning library that holds a vast collection of books, manuscripts, and research materials on Islamic art, history, and culture. The library serves as a valuable resource for scholars, researchers, and anyone seeking to delve deeper into the subject matter.

After immersing yourself in the mesmerizing world of Islamic art, take a moment to relax and enjoy the breathtaking views of Doha's skyline from the museum's terrace café. The serene setting, overlooking the azure waters of the Arabian Gulf, provides the perfect backdrop for reflection and contemplation.

The Museum of Islamic Art is not just a place for art appreciation; it is a sanctuary where the past and present converge, offering a glimpse into the beauty and diversity of Islamic civilization. It stands as a testament to Qatar's commitment to preserving its cultural heritage and sharing it with the world. A visit to this architectural gem is an enriching and enlightening experience that will leave you with a deep appreciation for the magnificence and enduring legacy of Islamic art.

The Corniche: A Picturesque Promenade Along Doha's Skyline

Stretching along the coastline of Doha, the Corniche is a scenic promenade that offers a breathtaking view of the city's skyline juxtaposed against the azure waters of the Arabian Gulf. This picturesque waterfront destination has become an iconic symbol of Doha, enticing locals and visitors alike to indulge in its beauty and tranquility.

The Corniche is a haven for leisure and recreation, attracting people from all walks of life. Whether you prefer a leisurely stroll, an invigorating jog, or a refreshing bike ride, the Corniche provides the perfect setting. The wide, paved pathways meander along the waterfront, inviting you to embark on a delightful journey of exploration and relaxation.

As you wander along the Corniche, your senses will be captivated by the panoramic vistas that unfold before you. On one side, you'll be treated to the impressive skyline of Doha, with its towering skyscrapers and architectural marvels. The modern cityscape, illuminated by the radiant Arabian sun, creates a striking contrast against the deep blue waters of the Gulf. On the other side, the Corniche is adorned with meticulously manicured green spaces, dotted with palm trees and vibrant flowers, creating a serene oasis in the heart of the city.

The Corniche is not just a place for physical activity; it is also a space for relaxation and rejuvenation. Along the promenade, you'll find numerous beautifully landscaped parks where you can unwind and immerse yourself in nature's embrace. Take a moment to recline on a bench, bask in the gentle sea breeze, and marvel at the natural beauty that surrounds you. These green havens provide a respite from the bustling city, allowing you to recharge and find solace in the tranquil ambiance.

For those seeking a culinary delight or a simple picnic, the Corniche offers an array of options. You can spread out a blanket on the grassy lawns and enjoy a leisurely picnic while gazing out at the shimmering waters of the Arabian Gulf. Alternatively, you can visit one of the many cafes and restaurants lining the promenade, offering a variety of delectable cuisines to satisfy your palate. From international flavors to local delicacies, the dining options along the Corniche cater to all tastes, ensuring a memorable culinary experience.

As the day transitions into evening, the Corniche transforms into a vibrant hub of activity. The setting sun paints the sky with hues of orange and pink, casting a warm glow over the city and the water. Locals and visitors flock to the Corniche during this magical time, creating a lively atmosphere filled with joy and excitement. Families gather for leisurely walks, children play in the parks, and couples relish romantic moments as they take in the enchanting views. The vibrant energy of the Corniche is infectious, enveloping everyone in its embrace and leaving lasting memories of Doha's captivating charm.

Beyond its visual splendor, the Corniche also hosts various events and festivals throughout the year. From cultural celebrations to sports activities, there is always something happening along this iconic promenade. The Corniche provides a platform for local talents to showcase their art, music, and traditions, adding an extra layer of cultural richness to the vibrant tapestry of Doha. Attending one of these events allows you to delve deeper into the essence of Qatar's heritage and community spirit. In addition to its recreational and cultural offerings, the Corniche promotes a healthy and active lifestyle. Fitness enthusiasts can take advantage of the dedicated jogging tracks and cycling lanes that run parallel to the promenade. Whether you're an avid runner, a cycling enthusiast, or simply looking to engage in some physical exercise, the Corniche provides a safe and scenic environment for your fitness endeavors.

As night falls, the Corniche continues to allure with its illuminated skyline. The modern architecture of Doha's skyline comes alive in a symphony of lights, casting a mesmerizing glow that reflects upon the tranquil waters. Take a leisurely stroll along the promenade, feeling the cool evening breeze caress your skin as you absorb the captivating beauty of the cityscape. The Corniche at night offers a serene and romantic ambiance, making it an ideal spot for couples to create lasting memories.

Aspire Tower: Sporting Excellence and Panoramic Views

Rising majestically above the cityscape, the Aspire Tower stands as an architectural marvel and a symbol of Qatar's unwavering passion for sports. Originally constructed for the 2006 Asian Games, this towering structure has become an iconic landmark in Doha, capturing the attention of visitors and locals alike. With its impressive height of 300 meters, the Aspire Tower offers breathtaking panoramic views of the city, providing a unique perspective on Doha's urban landscape.

One of the highlights of the Aspire Tower is its observation deck, which grants visitors a stunning vantage point to admire the city's beauty from above. As you ascend to the observation deck, you'll be treated to awe-inspiring vistas that stretch far beyond the city limits. The sprawling metropolis, the sparkling waters of the Arabian Gulf, and the surrounding desert landscape all come into view, creating a mesmerizing tableau of Qatar's diverse scenery.

From the observation deck, you can witness the vibrant tapestry of Doha's architectural wonders. The towering skyscrapers, such as the striking silhouette of the Doha skyline, are juxtaposed with traditional Qatari buildings and beautifully designed parks. The blend of modernity and heritage is evident from this aerial perspective, showcasing the city's continuous evolution and its commitment to preserving its cultural identity.

Beyond its architectural grandeur and stunning views, the Aspire Tower holds immense significance in promoting sporting excellence in Qatar. The tower's construction was closely tied to the 2006 Asian Games, a momentous event that marked Qatar's emergence as a global sports hub. The Asian Games showcased Qatar's dedication to hosting world-class sporting events, and the Aspire Tower played a crucial role in supporting these ambitions.

Designed to accommodate various sports facilities, the Aspire Tower stands as the centerpiece of the Aspire

Zone, a sprawling sports complex that encompasses state-of-the-art venues and training facilities. This impressive facility provides athletes with top-notch amenities to enhance their performance and prepare for international competitions. The Aspire Tower's towering presence serves as a constant reminder of Qatar's commitment to nurturing athletic talent and promoting sports as a vital aspect of the nation's identity.

Inside the tower, visitors can delve deeper into Qatar's sporting legacy by exploring the Aspire Academy. This renowned institution focuses on nurturing young athletes and honing their skills to compete at the highest level. The academy's commitment to developing talent and promoting sportsmanship has earned it recognition on the global stage. Visitors can gain insights into the academy's training programs, state-of-the-art facilities, and the successes achieved by its graduates.

Moreover, the Aspire Tower has become a venue for hosting international sporting events and conferences. Its multifunctional spaces have accommodated prestigious tournaments, symposiums, and exhibitions, attracting athletes, coaches, and sports enthusiasts from around the world. By welcoming such events, the tower further solidifies its position as a hub of athletic excellence and a testament to Qatar's dedication to fostering a sports culture that extends beyond its borders.

The Aspire Tower also embraces a commitment to sustainability. As part of Qatar's environmental initiatives, the tower incorporates innovative technologies to reduce its ecological footprint. From its energy-efficient design to its use of renewable energy sources, the tower showcases Qatar's determination to balance progress with environmental consciousness. By emphasizing sustainability, the Aspire Tower serves as a model for future architectural endeavors, reflecting the nation's holistic approach to development.

A visit to the Aspire Tower offers more than just a panoramic view of Doha; it provides an opportunity to witness Qatar's sporting achievements and its dedication to nurturing athletic talent. It stands as a testament to the nation's vision, passion, and commitment to hosting world-class sporting events. The tower's soaring presence and the awe-inspiring vistas from its observation deck encapsulate the essence of Doha's sporting spirit, inviting visitors to be part of Qatar's ongoing journey towards sporting excellence.

Sheikh Faisal Bin Qassim Al Thani Museum: A Unique Collection of Treasures

Nestled on the outskirts of Doha, away from the bustling city center, lies a hidden gem of cultural significance—the Sheikh Faisal Bin Qassim Al Thani Museum. This remarkable museum is a testament to Sheikh Faisal Bin Qassim Al Thani's dedication to preserving and sharing cultural heritage, as it showcases an extraordinary private collection spanning various epochs and civilizations.

As visitors enter the museum, they are immediately transported into a world of history and art. The vast exhibits offer a mesmerizing journey through time, with each artifact telling its own unique story. The collection encompasses an extensive range of items, including rare manuscripts, vintage cars, traditional Qatari handicrafts, and archaeological finds from around the world.

One of the notable highlights of the museum is its collection of rare manuscripts. These precious documents offer insights into ancient civilizations, showcasing the development of knowledge and the preservation of culture. Visitors can marvel at beautifully illuminated Qur'ans, ancient texts, and historical documents, gaining a deeper appreciation for the rich intellectual heritage of the region.

Moving through the museum, visitors encounter a captivating display of vintage cars. Sheikh Faisal Bin Qassim Al Thani's passion for automobiles is evident in the meticulously maintained collection of classic and rare vehicles. From sleek sports cars to elegant luxury automobiles, each car tells a story of innovation, design, and automotive history. This section of the museum offers a unique perspective on the evolution of transportation and showcases the beauty and craftsmanship of vintage automobiles.

The Sheikh Faisal Bin Qassim Al Thani Museum also serves as a tribute to Qatar's rich cultural traditions.

Traditional Qatari handicrafts are beautifully showcased, providing visitors with an insight into the skill and artistry of local artisans. Intricately woven carpets, delicate pottery, and exquisite jewelry highlight the craftsmanship that has been passed down through generations. This section of the museum celebrates the cultural heritage of Qatar, ensuring that these traditional arts and crafts continue to be appreciated and cherished.

In addition to the local treasures, the museum houses an impressive array of archaeological finds from various civilizations. Ancient artifacts from Mesopotamia, Egypt, Greece, and beyond offer a glimpse into the lives and achievements of civilizations long gone. Visitors can marvel at intricately carved statues, delicate pottery, and ancient tools, gaining a deeper understanding of the rich tapestry of human history.

Beyond the artifacts themselves, the museum's layout and design enhance the overall experience. The carefully curated exhibits are thoughtfully arranged, allowing visitors to explore each section at their own pace. Informative signage accompanies each display, providing historical context and enriching the visitor's understanding of the collection.

Moreover, the Sheikh Faisal Bin Qassim Al Thani Museum is not simply a static display of artifacts. It serves as a vibrant cultural center, hosting a variety of educational programs, workshops, and exhibitions throughout the year. Visitors have the opportunity to engage with experts, attend lectures, and participate in hands-on activities, further deepening their knowledge and appreciation of the collection and cultural heritage.

The museum's founder, Sheikh Faisal Bin Qassim Al Thani, is deeply committed to the preservation and sharing of cultural heritage. His passion for collecting and his dedication to education and cultural exchange have made this museum a beacon of knowledge and understanding. Through his efforts, the museum has become a bridge between the past and the present, fostering a greater appreciation for the diversity and beauty of world cultures.

Qatar National Library: A Hub of Knowledge and Culture

The Qatar National Library, situated in the heart of Doha, stands as a beacon of intellectual pursuits and cultural heritage. This magnificent facility, both in terms of its collection and architecture, is a testament to Qatar's commitment to knowledge and education. With its extensive collection of books, manuscripts, periodicals, and digital resources, the library serves as a haven for researchers, students, and bibliophiles alike.

Upon entering the Qatar National Library, visitors are immediately captivated by its stunning architecture. Designed by renowned Dutch architect Rem Koolhaas, in collaboration with Qatar-based firm OMA, the library's structure is a masterpiece of modern design. The building's geometric patterns and interplay of light and space create a visually striking environment that fosters a sense of curiosity and exploration.

The library's interior is equally impressive. Vast shelves lined with books of diverse subjects and languages fill the expansive halls, inviting visitors to embark on intellectual journeys. The collection spans a wide range of topics, from literature and history to science and technology, ensuring that there is something to pique the interest of every visitor. The library's commitment to multilingualism is evident, with books available in Arabic, English, and various other languages, reflecting Qatar's multicultural ethos.

In addition to its physical collection, the Qatar National Library embraces the digital age with its extensive digital resources. The library provides access to an array of online databases, e-books, and academic journals, ensuring that researchers have a wealth of information at their fingertips. State-of-the-art technology, including high-speed internet and multimedia facilities, further enhance the research capabilities of visitors, making the library a hub of innovation and learning.

Beyond its role as a repository of knowledge, the library serves as a vibrant center for intellectual exploration and cultural engagement. It hosts a wide range of cultural programs, exhibitions, and workshops that cater to diverse interests and age groups. Visitors can attend lectures by renowned scholars, participate in book clubs, or engage in interactive workshops on topics such as art, literature, and science. These events foster a sense of community and provide opportunities for individuals to exchange ideas, broaden their horizons, and deepen their understanding of the world.

One notable aspect of the Qatar National Library is its commitment to preserving and showcasing Qatar's cultural heritage. The library houses a special collection of rare manuscripts, historical documents, and artifacts that offer insights into Qatar's rich history and traditions. Visitors can explore the country's past through these precious artifacts, gaining a deeper appreciation for the cultural fabric of Qatar and the wider Arabian Peninsula.
The library's dedication to promoting research and scholarship extends beyond its physical walls. It actively collaborates with local and international institutions to facilitate research projects, academic conferences, and cultural exchanges. This spirit of collaboration positions the library as a vital contributor to the global academic community and enhances Qatar's standing as a hub for intellectual pursuits.

In addition to its academic and cultural endeavors, the Qatar National Library is also a space for leisure and relaxation. The library provides comfortable reading areas, quiet study rooms, and outdoor spaces where visitors can immerse themselves in books, engage in quiet contemplation, or simply enjoy the serene surroundings. The library's café offers a welcoming environment for individuals to connect over a cup of coffee, fostering a sense of community and camaraderie among visitors.

The Qatar National Library plays a crucial role in Qatar's vision for a knowledge-based society. It serves as a catalyst for intellectual growth, providing the resources, infrastructure, and opportunities for individuals to expand their knowledge and pursue their academic and cultural interests. The library's commitment to accessibility ensures that it is open to all, regardless of age, background, or academic affiliation.

In conclusion, the Qatar National Library stands as a remarkable institution that combines architectural splendor, a vast collection of resources, and a commitment to intellectual and cultural engagement. It is a place where individuals can delve into the world of knowledge, explore diverse subjects, and engage in meaningful discussions. Whether it is conducting research, attending cultural events, or simply finding solace in the world of books, the library offers a sanctuary for learning, discovery, and personal growth. As Qatar continues to nurture its position as a global hub for knowledge and innovation, the Qatar National Library remains a shining example of its unwavering dedication to intellectual pursuits and cultural preservation.

Embarking on a journey to explore these iconic landmarks will not only acquaint you with Doha's vibrant spirit but also provide a deeper understanding of Qatar's rich history, culture, and artistic treasures.

CHAPTER THREE

IMMERSING IN QATARI CULTURE

Qatar is a country deeply rooted in its traditions and customs, providing visitors with a unique opportunity to experience the rich cultural heritage of the Arabian Peninsula. In this chapter, we will explore various aspects of Qatari culture, including traditions and customs, the vibrant celebration of Qatar National Day, and the delectable flavors of traditional Qatari cuisine.

Qatari Traditions and Customs: Insights into Local Etiquette

When visiting Qatar, immersing oneself in the local customs and etiquette is crucial for a respectful and harmonious experience. Qataris have a rich cultural heritage and observing their social norms and traditions provides valuable insights into their way of life. By familiarizing yourself with these practices, you can gain a deeper understanding of the cultural fabric that shapes Qatari society.

One of the first aspects to consider is traditional greetings. Qataris place great importance on greetings as a way to show respect and establish a connection. The most common greeting is the Arabic phrase "As-salamu alaykum," which translates to "Peace be upon you." Responding with "Wa alaykum as-salam" demonstrates politeness and reciprocates the goodwill. Handshakes are also common among individuals of the same gender. However, it is important to note that in Qatari culture, men and women may have different greetings based on cultural considerations, so it's advisable to follow their lead.

Dress codes in Qatar are influenced by Islamic values and traditions. While Qatar is a modern and cosmopolitan country, it is respectful to dress modestly, especially in public places and religious sites. For women, loose-fitting clothing that covers the shoulders, arms, and legs is recommended. Wearing a headscarf (hijab) is not mandatory but may be appropriate in certain religious or formal settings. Men are expected to wear modest attire as well, avoiding revealing or tight-fitting clothing.

Hospitality is deeply ingrained in Qatari culture. Known as "arab hospitality," it is a cornerstone of social interactions. Qataris take pride in welcoming guests with warmth and generosity. When invited to a Qatari home, it is customary to remove your shoes before entering, as a sign of respect and cleanliness. Additionally, bringing a small gift, such as chocolates or flowers, is a thoughtful gesture to show appreciation for the hospitality extended to you.

The concept of majlis plays a significant role in Qatari society. A majlis is a dedicated space for socializing, discussions, and receiving guests. It is typically adorned with comfortable seating, cushions, and traditional Arabian hospitality. When attending a majlis, it is customary to follow the host's lead and be attentive to their guidance. Engaging in polite conversation, listening attentively, and showing interest in the topics being discussed are ways to demonstrate respect and appreciation for the opportunity to be part of the gathering.

Family holds immense importance in Qatari culture. The family unit is highly valued and serves as the foundation of society. Extended families often live in close proximity and maintain strong bonds. When interacting with Qatari families, it is important to respect their privacy and traditions. If invited to a family gathering, it is customary to bring a gift for the hosts and to show deference to elders. Qataris take pride in their family heritage, and discussions about family lineage and heritage are often welcomed as a way to connect and understand their roots.

Another aspect to consider is the significance of Ramadan, the holy month of fasting observed by Muslims worldwide. During this month, Qatar experiences a change in daily routines and practices.

Non-Muslim visitors should be aware of the cultural sensitivities surrounding Ramadan and should refrain from eating, drinking, or smoking in public during daylight hours as a sign of respect. It is also customary to greet Muslims with "Ramadan Kareem" or "Ramadan Mubarak" as an acknowledgment of the holy month.

Qatar National Day: Celebrating the Spirit of Qatar's Independence

Qatar National Day, celebrated on December 18th each year, is a momentous occasion that holds deep significance for the people of Qatar. It is a day that honors the country's rich history and commemorates its journey towards independence. This section delves into the significance of Qatar National Day, tracing its origins and exploring the various activities and events that take place across the nation. From captivating parades and cultural performances to fireworks displays and traditional dances, you will discover the true spirit of patriotism that permeates the air during this vibrant celebration.

Origins and Historical Significance

Qatar National Day marks the anniversary of Qatar's unification under the leadership of Sheikh Jassim bin Mohammed Al Thani, who became the ruler of the Qatari Peninsula in 1878. Prior to this unification, Qatar was composed of multiple tribes and villages, each with its own distinct identity. Sheikh Jassim's vision and leadership were instrumental in bringing these disparate regions together, forging a unified Qatari identity.

The Unification Process
The unification process, which culminated on December 18, 1878, involved negotiations and alliances among the various tribes and regions of Qatar. Sheikh Jassim's leadership and diplomatic skills were pivotal in creating a unified entity that would later evolve into the modern state of Qatar. The unification marked a turning point in Qatar's history, as it laid the foundation for the country's future growth, development, and independence.

Celebratory Atmosphere
Qatar National Day is a time of immense pride and joy for the people of Qatar, as they come together to celebrate their heritage and achievements. The entire country is adorned with Qatari flags, and the streets are filled with a festive spirit. The atmosphere is electric, with an air of anticipation and excitement palpable in every corner.

Parades and Processions
One of the most prominent features of Qatar National Day is the grand parade that takes place in the capital city of Doha. The parade showcases Qatar's rich cultural heritage and military prowess, with various military units, bands, and ceremonial displays participating in the procession. The parade route is lined with cheering crowds, waving flags, and applauding the participants as they pass by in a dazzling spectacle of color and pride.

Cultural Performances

Qatar National Day is an occasion for cultural expression, with a myriad of performances that showcase the artistic talents of Qatari nationals. Traditional dances, music, and theatrical performances take center stage, allowing visitors to immerse themselves in the beauty and richness of Qatari culture. From folk dances such as the Ardha (a traditional sword dance) to melodious tunes played on traditional instruments like the oud and tabla, the performances captivate audiences and provide a glimpse into the cultural heritage of Qatar.

Fireworks Displays

As evening descends, the night sky over Doha comes alive with breathtaking fireworks displays. The vibrant bursts of colors and patterns illuminate the cityscape, creating a dazzling spectacle that leaves spectators in awe. The fireworks symbolize the vibrancy, dynamism, and progress of Qatar as a nation, while also serving as a source of joy and celebration for all those in attendance.

Community Events and Festivities

Qatar National Day extends beyond the capital city, with celebrations taking place across the country. Various community events and festivities are organized in different regions, providing opportunities for locals and visitors alike to participate in the joyous celebrations. These events often include traditional sports competitions, camel races, falconry displays, and cultural exhibitions, offering a deeper immersion into Qatari traditions and customs.

Patriotic Displays
During Qatar National Day, Qataris proudly display their national pride and patriotism. Cars are adorned with Qatari flags, and buildings are adorned with decorative lighting and patriotic displays. The national colors of maroon and white dominate the visual landscape, creating a sense of unity and solidarity among the people. Qatar National Day serves as a reminder of the collective accomplishments and shared aspirations of the nation, fostering a sense of national unity and cohesion.

Meaningful Reflection and Gratitude
Qatar National Day is also a time for reflection and gratitude. It is an occasion to acknowledge the achievements and progress that Qatar has made over the years. It is a moment to appreciate the vision, resilience, and determination of the Qatari people in shaping their nation. Qatar National Day inspires gratitude for the opportunities and prosperity that the country has provided its citizens and residents, as well as gratitude for the rich cultural heritage that forms the bedrock of Qatari society.

Traditional Cuisine: Savoring the Flavors of Qatar's Culinary Delights

Qatari cuisine is a culinary tapestry woven with influences from the region's Bedouin heritage and its coastal location. It offers a delightful fusion of flavors, aromatic spices, and unique cooking techniques that have been passed down through generations. In this section, we invite you on a gastronomic journey to explore the rich and diverse culinary traditions of Qatar. From the renowned dishes of machboos and thareed to the indulgent sweetness of luqaimat, prepare to savor the hidden gems of Qatari cuisine.

Qatar's cuisine reflects its historical roots as a desert-dwelling society, where the Bedouins had to rely on simple yet flavorful ingredients to create nourishing meals. Spices such as cardamom, saffron, cinnamon, and turmeric play a vital role in Qatari cooking, infusing dishes with enticing aromas and distinct flavors. The Bedouin tradition of using local ingredients, combined with the influence of trade and neighboring countries, has shaped the diverse and vibrant Qatari culinary landscape.

One of the most iconic dishes in Qatari cuisine is machboos, a fragrant rice-based dish that exemplifies the fusion of flavors and cultural influences. Machboos is prepared by cooking long-grain rice with a blend of spices such as turmeric, cinnamon, and cardamom, then layering it with tenderly cooked meat or fish. The dish is often garnished with fried nuts and served with a side of tangy tomato sauce known as daqqus. Machboos showcases the mastery of Qatari chefs in balancing spices and creating a harmonious blend of tastes.

Another beloved dish that holds a special place in Qatari hearts is thareed. Considered a traditional comfort food, thareed is a hearty stew made with a combination of slow-cooked meat, fragrant vegetables, and aromatic spices. What sets thareed apart is the use of thin, handmade bread known as regag. The bread is torn into small pieces and soaked in the flavorsome broth until it softens, absorbing the rich flavors of the stew. Thareed is often enjoyed during Ramadan and other festive occasions, bringing families and friends together around a shared meal.

Qatar's coastal location also lends itself to a variety of seafood delights. From succulent grilled shrimp marinated in a blend of spices to delicate fish dishes infused with aromatic herbs, seafood plays a prominent role in Qatari cuisine. One popular seafood dish is majboos samak, where fish is marinated in a tangy spice mix and then cooked with rice, creating a mouthwatering harmony of flavors. The abundance of fresh seafood ensures that visitors to Qatar can indulge in a delectable array of dishes that highlight the natural bounty of the Arabian Gulf.

No culinary exploration of Qatar is complete without experiencing the delightful world of Qatari desserts. Among them, luqaimat takes center stage. These small, deep-fried dumplings are made from a simple batter of flour, yeast, sugar, and saffron, resulting in a crispy exterior and a soft, pillowy interior. Luqaimat are traditionally served drizzled with a sweet date syrup known as dibs, and their irresistible combination of textures and flavors makes them a popular choice for dessert or a sweet treat to accompany a cup of Qatari coffee.

While Qatari cuisine offers a tantalizing array of flavors, it is not just the dishes themselves that contribute to the immersive culinary experience. Traditional dining customs and the art of sharing meals are deeply rooted in Qatari culture. Qataris embrace the concept of communal dining, where meals are enjoyed together with family, friends, and even strangers. The dining table becomes a place of connection and celebration, where people bond over delicious food, engaging conversations, and heartfelt hospitality. During your journey in Qatar, you will have the opportunity to experience the warmth of Qatari hospitality and the joy of partaking in meals that bring people together.

In Qatari homes, it is common to find a large, communal platter known as a maseera at the center of the dining table. The maseera holds the main dish, and everyone gathers around it, using their right hand to share the food. This tradition emphasizes the value placed on unity, sharing, and building relationships through the act of dining together. As a guest, you will be welcomed with open arms, and sharing a meal with your Qatari hosts will offer an intimate glimpse into their culture and way of life.

Qatari Hospitality: The Art of Welcoming Guests

Hospitality holds great importance in Qatari culture, and visitors to Qatar are often overwhelmed by the warm and generous reception they receive. In this section, we will delve deeper into the concept of Qatari hospitality, known as "arab hospitality," and explore its significance in daily life. By understanding the customs, rituals, and etiquette associated with Qatari hospitality, you will gain valuable insights into the genuine warmth and kindness extended to guests in Qatar.

Qatari hospitality, deeply rooted in Bedouin traditions, reflects the strong sense of community, generosity, and respect that characterizes Qatari society. From the moment visitors set foot in Qatar, they are greeted with open arms and made to feel like honored guests. Qatari hospitality goes beyond mere politeness; it is a genuine expression of warmth and a way of forging meaningful connections.

One of the first experiences that showcases Qatari hospitality is the traditional welcome ritual. Upon arrival at a Qatari home, guests are greeted with "as-salam alaykum," which means "peace be upon you." This greeting sets the tone for the warm reception that follows. Guests are welcomed into the majlis, a designated room or area in the home specifically designed for socializing and receiving guests. The majlis is often adorned with comfortable seating, beautiful carpets, and ornate decorations, creating an inviting and relaxing atmosphere.

In the majlis, guests are treated to refreshments such as Arabic coffee (gahwa) and dates, which hold special significance in Qatari culture. Arabic coffee is traditionally served in small cups, and it is customary for guests to accept at least one cup as a gesture of appreciation. The host or a designated person, known as the "majlis master," serves the coffee, pouring it in a continuous stream from a long-spouted coffee pot called a dallah. This pouring method is symbolic, as it signifies the host's desire to continuously fill the cups of the guests.

During the gathering, conversation flows freely, and guests are encouraged to share their stories, experiences, and opinions. Qatari hosts are excellent conversationalists and take genuine interest in their guests, making them feel comfortable and engaged. It is common for lively discussions to take place on a wide range of topics, from local culture and traditions to global affairs.

As a guest, it is important to demonstrate respect and gratitude for the hospitality extended to you. Observing certain etiquettes will not only showcase your appreciation but also deepen the connection with your Qatari hosts. Here are a few key points to keep in mind:

Dress modestly: Qatari culture values modesty, so it is important to dress conservatively, especially when visiting someone's home. Women are advised to cover their shoulders and knees, and men should avoid wearing shorts.

Accept food and drink graciously: When offered food or drink, it is customary to accept graciously, even if you do not consume everything offered. Tasting a bit of each dish and expressing your enjoyment is a sign of appreciation.

Show respect for elders: Qatari society places great respect on elders. It is customary to greet elders first and offer them a seat of honor. When engaged in conversation, listen attentively and demonstrate respect for their wisdom and experience.

Remove your shoes: When entering a Qatari home, it is customary to remove your shoes. This practice helps maintain cleanliness and shows respect for the host's space.

Express gratitude: Throughout your visit, express your gratitude for the hospitality extended to you. A heartfelt thank-you at the end of the gathering goes a long way in acknowledging the efforts made by your hosts.

Consider bringing a gift: While not mandatory, bringing a small gift as a token of appreciation is a thoughtful gesture. Traditional gifts such as dates, Arabic sweets, or a souvenir from your home country are often well-received.

By following these etiquettes, you will demonstrate your respect for Qatari customs and traditions, and your hosts will appreciate your efforts to embrace their culture. Qatari hospitality is reciprocal, and your hosts will likely go above and beyond to ensure your comfort and enjoyment.

It is worth noting that Qatari hospitality extends beyond the home. When exploring public spaces, such as markets or traditional souqs, visitors will find that shopkeepers and vendors also embody the spirit of hospitality. They greet customers warmly, offer assistance, and may even invite you to partake in a cup of tea while you browse their wares. Embracing these interactions and engaging in genuine conversations can lead to memorable encounters and insights into local life.

Qatari hospitality is a testament to the genuine warmth and generosity of the Qatari people. By immersing yourself in the customs and practices of Qatari hospitality, you will not only forge meaningful connections but also gain a deeper appreciation for the culture and traditions that shape Qatar. So, embrace the spirit of "arab hospitality" and allow yourself to be captivated by the genuine warmth and kindness that awaits you in Qatar.

Traditional Arts and Crafts: Preserving Cultural Heritage

Qatar has a rich artistic heritage that spans centuries and is deeply intertwined with its culture and traditions. This vibrant artistic legacy encompasses various forms of creative expression, from the intricate art of calligraphy to the craftsmanship of hand-woven carpets and textiles, as well as the symbolism behind traditional jewelry and garments. This section will take you on a captivating journey through the world of traditional Qatari arts and crafts, providing insights into their historical significance, cultural relevance, and the efforts made to preserve and promote them.

One of the most revered art forms in Qatar is calligraphy, an ancient practice that holds great importance in Islamic art and culture. Islamic calligraphy is a visual representation of the Quranic verses and teachings, and it has been perfected over centuries by master calligraphers. In Qatar, calligraphy can be seen adorning mosques, palaces, and public spaces, showcasing the skill and precision of Qatari artisans. From the flowing curves of thuluth script to the geometric intricacies of kufic script, each style of calligraphy carries its own unique beauty and symbolism. By delving into the art of calligraphy, you will gain an appreciation for the dedication and mastery required to create these exquisite works of art.

The art of hand-woven carpets and textiles is another cornerstone of Qatari craftsmanship. Qatari carpets are renowned for their intricate designs, vibrant colors, and superior quality. These carpets often feature geometric patterns, floral motifs, and representations of animals, showcasing the cultural influences and historical narratives that have shaped Qatari society. Traditional Qatari textiles, such as the embroidered sadu fabric, also hold significant cultural value. Sadu weaving is a traditional craft practiced by Qatari women, where intricate patterns are meticulously woven into textiles using a wooden loom. These textiles often depict desert landscapes, camels, and other elements inspired by Qatari heritage. Exploring the world of Qatari carpets and textiles will allow you to appreciate the skill and artistry behind these timeless creations.

In addition to calligraphy and textiles, traditional Qatari jewelry and garments are rich in symbolism and cultural significance. Qatari jewelry often features intricate designs adorned with precious gemstones, reflecting the country's historical connections to the pearl trade and the Arabian Gulf's natural resources. These pieces of jewelry are not only decorative but also carry symbolic meanings, representing social status, marital status, and cultural identity. Qatari garments, such as the thobe (traditional men's robe) and abaya (women's cloak), showcase the blending of tradition and modernity. While these garments retain their traditional elements, they also reflect contemporary fashion trends, incorporating innovative designs and luxurious fabrics. By exploring the symbolism behind traditional Qatari jewelry and garments, you will gain a deeper understanding of the cultural narratives and values they represent.

Qatar's commitment to preserving its cultural heritage and promoting artistic expression is evident in various initiatives and institutions throughout the country. One notable example is the Sheikh Faisal Bin Qassim Al Thani Museum, a treasure trove of Qatari artifacts and a hub for cultural exchange and education. The museum showcases a diverse collection that spans Islamic art, archaeology, heritage items, and vintage vehicles. Visitors can explore the vast array of exhibits, including intricately crafted calligraphy pieces, traditional textiles, and exquisite jewelry, gaining a comprehensive understanding of Qatar's artistic heritage. The museum's commitment to education and cultural exchange is exemplified through its various programs and events, which aim to engage visitors of all ages and backgrounds in learning about Qatari culture and traditions.

Furthermore, Qatar has been investing in the promotion of traditional arts and crafts through festivals, workshops, and exhibitions. These platforms provide opportunities for local artisans to showcase their skills and talents, while also fostering a deeper appreciation for Qatari art and culture among both residents and visitors. By attending these events, you can witness firsthand the creativity and dedication of Qatari artists and craftsmen, as well as engage in interactive workshops to learn traditional techniques and create your own masterpieces.

By immersing yourself in Qatari culture, you will gain a profound appreciation for the country's heritage, values, and way of life. Whether engaging in conversations with locals, participating in traditional festivities, or savoring the flavors of authentic Qatari cuisine, this chapter will equip you with the knowledge and insights necessary to fully embrace the cultural tapestry that makes Qatar a truly captivating destination.

CHAPTER FOUR

DAY TRIPS FROM DOHA

While Doha itself offers a myriad of attractions and activities, venturing beyond the city limits unveils a world of captivating landscapes, cultural treasures, and natural wonders. Qatar's strategic location on the Arabian Peninsula makes it an ideal hub for day trips that provide a diverse range of experiences. From historic forts and stunning desert landscapes to picturesque islands and traditional fishing villages, these day trips offer an opportunity to discover the hidden gems of Qatar.

Exploring the Desert: Adventures in the Inland Sea and Khor Al Udeid

Embark on an exhilarating day trip from Doha to explore the mesmerizing desert landscapes surrounding the city. Just a short drive away, you'll discover two stunning destinations: the Inland Sea and Khor Al Udeid.

The Inland Sea, also known as Khor Al Adaid, is a natural wonder nestled in the heart of the Qatari desert. As you venture into this remote area, prepare to be awe-struck by the breathtaking sight of towering sand dunes meeting the tranquil waters of the Arabian Gulf. The journey itself is an adventure as you traverse through the desert, witnessing the dramatic shift in terrain and immersing yourself in the vastness of the dunes.

Once you arrive at the Inland Sea, a sense of tranquility envelopes you. The pristine waters of the Arabian Gulf gently lap against the shore, creating a serene atmosphere that contrasts with the ruggedness of the surrounding desert. Take a moment to relax and soak in the beauty of the landscape, allowing the stillness to rejuvenate your spirit.

For those seeking an adrenaline rush, dune bashing is a must-do activity in the Inland Sea. Skilled drivers navigate the undulating sands in powerful 4x4 vehicles, offering an exhilarating and heart-pounding experience. Hold on tight as you race up and down the dunes, feeling the adrenaline coursing through your veins. The combination of high-speed thrills and the stunning desert scenery creates an unforgettable adventure.

After the excitement of dune bashing, it's time to unwind and enjoy the serenity of the Inland Sea. Take a dip in the crystal-clear waters, refreshing yourself in nature's own oasis. The calmness of the sea provides the perfect opportunity for swimming, snorkeling, or simply floating leisurely. As you submerge yourself in the cool waters, surrounded by the golden sands and the vastness of the desert, you'll experience a sense of peace and harmony with the natural world.

To enhance your experience, consider indulging in a serene beachside picnic. Spread out a blanket on the soft sands and savor a delicious meal amidst this idyllic setting. Whether it's a homemade feast or a carefully prepared picnic basket, the combination of delectable food and breathtaking scenery elevates your dining experience to new heights. As you enjoy your meal, the sounds of the gentle waves and the whispering desert breeze create a symphony of nature, enhancing the sense of tranquility and contentment.

Continuing your day trip, venture to Khor Al Udeid, also known as the "Inland Sea" due to its similar natural formation. This unique body of water, surrounded by golden dunes, creates a picturesque backdrop for a range of activities. As you arrive at Khor Al Udeid, you'll be captivated by the striking beauty of the landscape.

For thrill-seekers and adventure enthusiasts, sandboarding is a popular activity in Khor Al Udeid. Strap on a sandboard and glide down the slopes of the dunes, experiencing the exhilaration of surfing the desert. Feel the rush of the wind against your face as you navigate the sandy slopes, creating your own tracks in the soft, untouched sand. It's a thrilling and unforgettable experience that combines the excitement of snowboarding with the unique charm of the desert.

Another iconic activity in Khor Al Udeid is camel riding. Embark on a journey across the vast expanse of golden sands, accompanied by these gentle and majestic creatures. As you sway with the rhythmic motion of the camel's gait, you'll feel a deep connection with the heritage and traditions of the desert. The vastness of the desert stretches out before you, and the ever-changing patterns of the sand create a mesmerizing landscape that leaves a lasting impression.

As you explore Khor Al Udeid, keep your camera at the ready to capture the beauty of the desert. The shifting sunlight casts a magical glow over the landscape, creating a play of shadows and highlights that transform the dunes into a work of art. From sunrise to sunset, each moment presents a new and captivating scene, inviting you to capture the essence of this unique destination through photography.

Al Zubarah Archaeological Site: Tracing Qatar's Ancient History

Delve into the rich history of Qatar with a day trip to the Al Zubarah Archaeological Site, a UNESCO World Heritage site that offers a fascinating glimpse into the country's ancient past. Located approximately 105 kilometers northwest of Doha, this well-preserved archaeological site provides a captivating insight into the once-thriving pearl trading and fishing port of Al Zubarah.

As you embark on your journey from Doha to Al Zubarah, you'll be transported back in time to an era when this coastal town flourished as a prominent trading hub. The journey itself is an opportunity to appreciate Qatar's diverse landscapes, as you pass by picturesque desert dunes and expansive coastal plains. Upon arrival at

Al Zubarah, you'll be greeted by the awe-inspiring sight of the archaeological site, set against the backdrop of the azure Arabian Gulf.

Step into the past as you explore the extensive ruins of Al Zubarah. Marvel at the remnants of fortifications, city walls, and residential structures that once thrived with bustling activity. The architectural layout and design of the site provide valuable insights into the urban planning and defensive strategies of the 18th and 19th centuries.

Wander through the reconstructed buildings, carefully restored to showcase the daily life and culture of the time. Visit the mosque, a place of worship that served as a central gathering point for the community. Admire the intricate details of the courtyard houses, which housed families and reflected the traditional Qatari architectural style. As you enter a traditional Qatari majlis, a communal space for social gatherings, let your imagination transport you to a time when lively conversations and important decisions unfolded within these walls.

One of the highlights of your visit is the on-site museum, which further enhances your understanding of Al Zubarah's significance in Qatar's history. The museum's exhibition showcases a fascinating collection of artifacts unearthed from the site, providing a tangible connection to the past. Explore the displays of pottery, jewelry, and weaponry, each item telling a story of the town's vibrant trading culture and maritime heritage.

The Al Zubarah Archaeological Site also offers the opportunity to grasp the region's strategic importance in the maritime trade network. As you wander among the ruins, you'll gain a deeper appreciation for the challenges and triumphs faced by the pearl traders and fishermen who once called Al Zubarah home. The strategic location of the town facilitated its connection with neighboring countries in the Gulf region, allowing for the exchange of goods, ideas, and cultural influences.

Beyond the historical significance, the Al Zubarah Archaeological Site is a testament to the dedication and efforts of conservationists and archaeologists. The meticulous preservation and ongoing research conducted at the site contribute to the collective understanding of Qatar's past and its place within the broader historical narrative of the Arabian Peninsula.

To make the most of your visit, consider joining a guided tour led by knowledgeable experts who can provide further context and insights into the site's significance. Their expertise will bring the ruins to life, allowing you to appreciate the intricate details and historical context of the structures that have withstood the test of time.

As you conclude your day trip to the Al Zubarah Archaeological Site, take a moment to reflect on the immense historical value of this UNESCO World Heritage site. The town of Al Zubarah, once a thriving center of trade and cultural exchange, now stands as a testament to Qatar's rich heritage and its role in shaping the region's history. The experience of exploring the ruins, wandering through reconstructed buildings, and immersing yourself in the exhibits at the museum will leave you with a deeper appreciation for the cultural legacy that has shaped modern-day Qatar.

Umm Salal Mohammed Fort: A Glimpse into Qatari Heritage

Journey back in time and discover the historic Umm Salal Mohammed Fort, located just a short distance from Doha. This fort, believed to have been constructed in the late 19th century, provides a captivating insight into Qatari heritage and architectural traditions.

As you approach Umm Salal Mohammed Fort, you'll be greeted by its impressive walls, standing as a testament to Qatar's rich history. Stepping inside the fort's entrance, you'll be transported to a bygone era, where you can explore the well-preserved rooms, corridors, and courtyards that once served as living quarters for the local ruling family. The fort's architecture reflects traditional Qatari design elements, showcasing the ingenuity and craftsmanship of the time.

Admire the traditional architectural elements that make Umm Salal Mohammed Fort a unique cultural gem. The fort features wind towers, known as "barjeel," strategically placed to catch the gentle breeze and provide natural ventilation, keeping the interiors cool in the harsh desert climate. These architectural marvels are a prime example of how Qatari ancestors ingeniously harnessed nature to create comfortable living spaces.

As you explore the fort, take the time to appreciate the intricate wooden doors and windows that adorn its rooms. The skilled craftsmanship and detailed carvings showcase the artistry and attention to detail that were highly valued in Qatari architecture. These decorative elements serve as a testament to the cultural significance of aesthetics in Qatari heritage.

The fort's courtyards offer a peaceful and serene atmosphere, inviting you to take a leisurely stroll and immerse yourself in the ambiance of the past. The beautifully landscaped gardens, with their lush greenery and vibrant flowers, create a tranquil oasis within the fort's walls. Pause to appreciate the serene surroundings and listen to the gentle rustle of the wind through the palm trees. The combination of natural beauty and architectural splendor creates a captivating atmosphere that invites reflection and contemplation.

As you wander through Umm Salal Mohammed Fort, let your imagination transport you to the events and stories that unfolded within these walls. Picture the bustling activity of daily life as the ruling family and their entourage resided in these quarters. Envision the vibrant social gatherings and the important decisions that were made in these historic chambers. The fort's rich history comes alive as you immerse yourself in its well-preserved spaces.

Beyond the fort's walls, you'll find expansive open spaces that further add to the charm of Umm Salal Mohammed Fort. These areas provide an opportunity to connect with nature while exploring the fort's surroundings. The carefully manicured gardens, adorned with local flora, create a harmonious blend of beauty and history. Find a quiet spot to sit and absorb the tranquil atmosphere, allowing yourself to be transported back in time.

Umm Salal Mohammed Fort is not just a physical structure; it represents a significant chapter in Qatar's history. Visiting this historical site offers a unique opportunity to gain a deeper appreciation for the country's rich cultural heritage. The fort serves as a reminder of Qatar's past, preserving its traditions and architectural legacy for future generations to cherish.

As you leave Umm Salal Mohammed Fort, carry with you the memories of its timeless beauty and the insights gained into Qatari heritage. Reflect on the fort's significance in shaping the identity of Qatar and its people. Umm Salal Mohammed Fort stands as a testament to the resilience and ingenuity of a nation, encapsulating the spirit of the past while embracing the present.

Immersing yourself in the historic Umm Salal Mohammed Fort is a journey that transcends time. It invites you to connect with the past, appreciate the present, and gain a deeper understanding of Qatar's cultural tapestry. Whether you are a history enthusiast, an architecture aficionado, or simply a curious traveler, this fort offers an unforgettable experience that will leave an indelible mark on your journey through Qatar.

Zekreet Peninsula and Film City: Immerse Yourself in Qatar's Film Culture

Embark on a day trip to the scenic Zekreet Peninsula, located west of Doha, and immerse yourself in the fascinating world of Film City. As you venture into this unique destination, you'll find yourself transported to a surreal landscape that has served as the backdrop for numerous film productions, creating an atmosphere of mystery and enchantment.

Zekreet Peninsula is a hidden gem that offers a captivating blend of natural beauty and cinematic history. Upon arrival, you'll be greeted by vast stretches of rugged terrain, dotted with intriguing rock formations and an otherworldly ambiance. The peninsula's unique geological features have made it an ideal location for filmmakers, attracting both international and local productions to capture its captivating allure on the silver screen.

The centerpiece of Zekreet Peninsula is the captivating Film City, an abandoned village constructed specifically for movie sets. As you explore the deserted streets, you'll feel a sense of stepping into another world, where captivating stories were once brought to life. The meticulously crafted sets, including a replica of an Arabian village, allow you to immerse yourself in the ambiance of ancient times and imagine the dramatic scenes that unfolded within these walls. The attention to detail is remarkable, from the intricately carved doors to the weathered textures that lend an air of authenticity to the surroundings.

As you wander through the abandoned film sets, take the opportunity to unleash your imagination and envision yourself as a character in your own cinematic tale. The silence of the deserted streets allows you to appreciate the artistry and craftsmanship that went into creating these temporary worlds. Capture the magic of the moment through photography, preserving memories that reflect the unique fusion of reality and fiction.

Beyond the film sets, Zekreet Peninsula offers a rugged and picturesque coastline that stretches along the Arabian Gulf. Take a leisurely walk along the sandy shores, feeling the warm embrace of the sea breeze and reveling in the tranquility of the surroundings. The rocky formations that emerge from the sandy landscape add an element of drama and provide the perfect backdrop for capturing stunning photographs. Be sure to keep an eye out for the diverse marine life that inhabits the area, as dolphins can occasionally be spotted frolicking in the azure waters.

For those seeking a more adventurous experience, Zekreet Peninsula offers the opportunity to explore its hidden caves and caverns. These natural formations have been carved over time by the relentless forces of wind and water, resulting in an intricate network of tunnels and chambers. Embark on a thrilling underground adventure, guided by experienced professionals who can lead you through this captivating subterranean world. Discover the secrets that lie beneath the surface and witness the remarkable geological formations up close.

As you conclude your day trip to Zekreet Peninsula, take a moment to reflect on the unique blend of natural beauty and cinematic history that defines this captivating destination. The surreal landscape, abandoned film sets, and breathtaking coastline combine to create an experience that is both awe-inspiring and unforgettable. Whether you're a film enthusiast, a nature lover, or simply someone seeking a unique adventure, Zekreet Peninsula and Film City offer a remarkable journey into a world where reality and imagination intertwine. Allow yourself to be captivated by the enchantment of this hidden gem and create memories that will last a lifetime.

North Qatar Mangroves and Al Khor City: Nature's Hidden Oasis

Escape the bustling city and delve into the serene beauty of the North Qatar Mangroves. Nestled along the coastline, just a short drive from Doha, this hidden oasis offers a tranquil retreat from the urban hustle and bustle.

Embarking on a day trip to the mangroves promises an enchanting journey through nature's wonders and a chance to immerse yourself in Qatar's rich ecological diversity.

To fully appreciate the North Qatar Mangroves, it's highly recommended to join a guided tour or rent a kayak for an up-close and personal exploration. As you paddle through the calm waters, you'll find yourself surrounded by a labyrinth of mangrove channels, where lush greenery thrives in the brackish waters. The towering mangrove trees, with their intricate root systems, create a mesmerizing landscape and provide a crucial habitat for a wide array of wildlife.

One of the highlights of the mangroves is the opportunity to observe migratory birds that flock to this haven, seeking refuge and sustenance during their long journeys. Keep your eyes peeled for graceful herons, elegant flamingos, and other avian species that make this area their temporary home. The symphony of bird calls adds to the serene ambiance, creating a peaceful backdrop for your exploration.

As you navigate through the mangroves, you'll also encounter an abundance of marine life. Watch in awe as fiddler crabs scuttle along the muddy banks, their vibrant colors adding a touch of whimsy to the scenery. The shallow waters teem with fish, while the occasional glimpse of a shy sea turtle or a curious dolphin can be a magical encounter. The mangroves provide a sanctuary for these creatures, offering them shelter and nourishment in a unique ecosystem.

The North Qatar Mangroves serve as a living testament to the importance of conservation efforts. It is a fragile ecosystem that relies on a delicate balance of tides, freshwater inflows, and salinity levels. Various organizations and local initiatives work tirelessly to protect and preserve this natural treasure, ensuring its sustainability for future generations.

After your serene mangrove experience, continue your day trip by visiting Al Khor City, a charming coastal town located nearby. Renowned for its traditional dhow boatyards and vibrant fish market, Al Khor offers a glimpse into Qatar's seafaring heritage and a chance to immerse yourself in the local atmosphere.

Stroll along the waterfront promenade, where you'll witness the proud craftsmanship of the dhow boat builders. These traditional wooden vessels, with their distinctive curved shapes and intricately carved details, are an integral part of Qatar's maritime traditions. Marvel at the skill and dedication of the craftsmen as they meticulously construct these seafaring beauties, carrying on a legacy that stretches back through generations.

The heart of Al Khor City lies in its bustling fish market, where the aromas of the sea mingle with the vibrant colors of freshly caught seafood. This vibrant market is a hub of activity, with local fishermen showcasing their bounties of the day. Engage with the friendly vendors, who are more than happy to share their knowledge and passion for the sea. Learn about different fish species, traditional fishing techniques, and the importance of sustainable fishing practices in the region.

Indulge in the flavors of the sea by sampling the freshest seafood dishes available. From succulent prawns and juicy fish to delectable grilled squid, the culinary offerings are a true delight for seafood lovers. Enjoy a traditional Qatari meal at one of the local restaurants, where the dishes are prepared with expertise and showcase the rich flavors of the Arabian Gulf.

Al Khor City also offers opportunities to delve deeper into Qatar's seafaring heritage. Visit the Al Khor Museum, where you can learn about the history of the town and its connection to the sea. Discover artifacts, photographs, and exhibits that provide insights into the traditional way of life and the impact of fishing on the local community.

As your day trip draws to a close, take a moment to soak in the relaxed ambiance of Al Khor City. Enjoy a leisurely walk along the picturesque Corniche, where traditional dhows gently bob in the harbor and the sea breeze caresses your face. The stunning views of the Gulf and the distant horizon create a sense of serenity, allowing you to reflect on the natural beauty and cultural heritage you have experienced throughout the day.

The day trip to the North Qatar Mangroves and Al Khor City is a perfect blend of nature, culture, and heritage. It provides a refreshing escape from the city and a chance to connect with the natural wonders of Qatar. If you are a nature enthusiast, a history buff, or simply seeking a peaceful retreat, this day trip promises to leave you with lasting memories and a deep appreciation for the ecological and cultural treasures that Qatar has to offer.

Sheikh Faisal Museum and Camel Race Track: Cultural and Sporting Adventures

Embark on a cultural and sporting day trip by visiting the Sheikh Faisal Museum and the nearby camel race track. This immersive journey will take you deep into Qatari heritage, offering a glimpse into the rich history and traditional sporting events that have shaped the country's culture.

Begin your adventure at the Sheikh Faisal Museum, situated in Al Samriya, a short drive from Doha. This extraordinary museum houses an extensive collection of artifacts that span various facets of Qatari heritage. As you step into the museum, you'll be greeted by a captivating display of vintage cars and historic aircraft, showcasing Qatar's connection to the world of transportation. Admire the sleek curves and elegant designs of classic automobiles, each with its own story to tell. Marvel at the sight of vintage aircraft suspended from the ceiling, evoking a sense of nostalgia for a bygone era of aviation.

Continuing your exploration, immerse yourself in the intricate beauty of traditional Qatari handicrafts. Intricately woven textiles, vibrant carpets, and ornate wooden furniture adorned with delicate carvings are among the treasures that await you. These crafts reflect the skilled craftsmanship and artistic expressions deeply rooted in Qatari culture. Allow yourself to be transported back in time as you appreciate the meticulous details and the stories behind each masterpiece.

The museum also boasts a remarkable collection of Islamic art, showcasing the beauty and diversity of this rich artistic tradition. Marvel at the intricately designed calligraphy, delicate ceramics, and exquisite manuscripts that demonstrate the mastery of Islamic artists throughout history. Explore the spiritual significance of these artistic expressions, gaining a deeper understanding of the role of art in Islamic culture.

After immersing yourself in the wealth of cultural artifacts, it's time to head to the camel race track, located nearby. Camel racing holds a special place in Qatari culture, representing a centuries-old tradition that has evolved into a thrilling sporting spectacle. As you approach the race track, you'll sense the anticipation and excitement in the air.

Camel racing in Qatar is a unique and exhilarating experience that showcases the country's deep connection to its Bedouin heritage. Camels, the "ships of the desert," are revered animals and have played a vital role in Qatari life for centuries. The races take place in specially designed tracks, where camels, guided by skilled jockeys, compete for victory.

Take a seat in the grandstands, surrounded by enthusiastic spectators, and feel the thrill as the camels thunder down the track. The rhythmic sound of their hooves pounding the sand echoes through the air, creating an electric atmosphere. Witness the sheer speed and agility of these majestic creatures as they compete against each other, driven by their natural instinct and the encouragement of their jockeys.

Camel racing is not just a sporting event; it is deeply ingrained in Qatari culture. The races bring communities together, fostering a sense of camaraderie and celebration. Attendees from all walks of life gather to witness the spectacle, cheering on their favorite camels and reveling in the joy of this traditional sport.

As you watch the races unfold, gain insights into the significance of camel racing in Qatari culture. Learn about the meticulous training and care that goes into preparing the camels for these events. Discover the history and traditions associated with camel racing, from its roots in Bedouin society to its modern-day adaptation.

A day trip that combines a visit to the Sheikh Faisal Museum and the camel race track offers a multifaceted experience. It allows you to immerse yourself in the cultural heritage of Qatar, appreciating the art, craftsmanship, and history that have shaped the country. Simultaneously, it provides an opportunity to witness the excitement and tradition of camel racing, connecting with the essence of Qatari society.

Through this journey, you'll gain a deeper appreciation for Qatar's cultural richness and the profound bond between its people and the land. It's an adventure that will leave you with lasting memories, a greater understanding of Qatari heritage, and a sense of awe for the majestic camels that have been an integral part of the country's identity for centuries.

These day trips from Doha provide a diverse range of experiences, from thrilling desert adventures to immersive historical journeys. Whether you seek adrenaline-pumping activities or a deeper understanding of Qatar's heritage, these destinations promise unforgettable experiences and memories to cherish.

CHAPTER FIVE

OUTDOOR RECREATION AND NATURAL WONDERS

Doha a captivating city where outdoor recreation and natural wonders intertwine to create a truly unique experience. Amidst the modern skyline and bustling streets, Doha reveals a wealth of opportunities to connect with nature and indulge in exciting outdoor activities.

Aspire Park: Serenity and Greenery in the Heart of Doha

Located in the heart of Doha, Aspire Park is a breathtaking oasis that offers serenity and abundant greenery amidst the bustling cityscape. Spanning over 88 hectares, this expansive park is a haven for nature lovers and those seeking a peaceful retreat.

Aspire Park features meticulously manicured lawns, vibrant flower beds, and scenic walking paths that wind through its lush landscapes. The park's meticulous maintenance and attention to detail make it a visual feast for visitors. Whether you're taking a leisurely stroll, having a picnic, or simply enjoying the fresh air, the park's green surroundings create a tranquil ambiance that allows you to escape the urban hustle and immerse yourself in nature's embrace.

The park's centerpiece is the iconic Torch Tower, a striking landmark that offers panoramic views of Doha's skyline. Aspire Park's strategic location adjacent to the Torch Tower allows visitors to witness the city's architectural marvels while being surrounded by natural beauty. The tower's impressive height and sleek design make it a distinctive feature of the park's landscape, adding to the allure and grandeur of the surroundings.

Adjacent to Aspire Park is the sprawling Aspire Zone, a sports complex that further enhances the park's appeal. Aspire Zone offers state-of-the-art sports facilities, including a football stadium, indoor arenas, and outdoor tracks. This combination of a tranquil park and a world-class sports complex creates a harmonious blend of recreational activities for visitors of all ages. Whether you're a sports enthusiast looking to engage in a game or a spectator cheering on your favorite team, Aspire Zone provides a vibrant atmosphere that adds to the park's overall charm.

Families and friends often gather at Aspire Park for picnics, leisurely strolls, or energetic outdoor activities. The park's ample facilities cater to diverse interests, ensuring there's something for everyone. Children can enjoy playgrounds equipped with swings, slides, and climbing structures, while sports enthusiasts can make use of the various sports courts for basketball, tennis, and volleyball. Jogging tracks meander through the park, providing a scenic path for runners and walkers to stay active while immersing themselves in nature's beauty.

Visitors can also rent bicycles from designated rental stations within the park. Cycling through the park's pathways offers a fun and eco-friendly way to explore its expansive grounds. Additionally, group fitness classes, such as yoga and aerobics, are organized within the park, providing opportunities for visitors to engage in invigorating workouts while enjoying the serene surroundings.

For those seeking tranquility, Aspire Park offers secluded areas with cozy benches and shaded spots. These peaceful corners provide a perfect retreat for individuals looking to unwind, read a book, or simply find solace in nature. The park's design incorporates elements of privacy and seclusion, allowing visitors to find their own little pockets of tranquility amidst the expansive greenery.

One of the highlights of Aspire Park is its serene lake, which adds to the park's soothing ambiance. The lake is adorned with fountains and charming bridges that enhance the scenic beauty of the surroundings. Visitors can sit by the lake, listen to the gentle sounds of flowing water, and watch the graceful movement of the fountains. The lake's tranquil atmosphere creates a sense of calm and serenity, providing a space for contemplation and reflection.

With its well-maintained facilities and serene atmosphere, Aspire Park serves as a popular venue for events and gatherings throughout the year. The park hosts various community festivals, cultural celebrations, and live performances that bring the local community together. These events showcase the rich diversity of Doha's culture and provide an opportunity for people to connect, share experiences, and celebrate in a vibrant and inclusive environment. The park's open spaces and beautiful surroundings provide an ideal setting for such gatherings, fostering a sense of unity and togetherness among residents and visitors alike.

In summary, Aspire Park offers a remarkable blend of natural beauty and modern amenities. It provides a sanctuary of serenity and greenery in the heart of Doha, where visitors can escape the city's hustle and bustle and find solace in nature's embrace. With its meticulously manicured landscapes, well-maintained facilities, and tranquil atmosphere, Aspire Park is a haven for relaxation, recreation, and community engagement.

Sealine Beach Resort: Sun, Sand, and Sea on Qatar's Eastern Coast

Located along Qatar's mesmerizing eastern coast, Sealine Beach Resort offers a blissful escape from the urban hustle and bustle, providing a perfect blend of sun, sand, and sea. Nestled amidst picturesque sand dunes, this beachfront resort is a paradise for beach lovers and water enthusiasts.

Sealine Beach Resort sits on a pristine coastline that stretches as far as the eye can see, inviting visitors to indulge in sun-soaked relaxation or engage in various water activities. The resort offers a wide range of water sports, catering to all levels of thrill-seekers. Whether it's jet skiing, kayaking, or paddleboarding, guests can explore the azure waters of the Arabian Gulf and experience the thrill of gliding across the waves.

The expansive sandy beach at Sealine Beach Resort provides ample space for sunbathing, building sandcastles, or simply taking a leisurely stroll along the shoreline. As the warm sun caresses your skin and the gentle sea breeze whispers through your hair, you'll find yourself immersed in a serene atmosphere that washes away the stresses of everyday life. The breathtaking views of the endless horizon and the gentle lapping of the waves create an idyllic setting for relaxation and rejuvenation.

Sealine Beach Resort is not only a haven for relaxation but also a hub of adventure. For those seeking an adrenaline rush, the resort organizes thrilling desert safaris and dune bashing experiences. Hop aboard a sturdy 4x4 vehicle and embark on an exhilarating ride across the golden sand dunes, feeling the adrenaline surge through your veins as the vehicle conquers the steep slopes and twists through the sandy terrain. The breathtaking desert landscape unfolds before your eyes, offering a sense of awe and wonder.

If you prefer a more traditional desert experience, camel rides are available, allowing you to leisurely traverse the dunes while embracing the slower pace of life. Feel the gentle sway of the camel's gait as you soak in the peaceful ambiance of the desert. Alternatively, quad biking adventures provide an opportunity to immerse yourself in the unique desert environment at a faster pace. Zoom across the sand, navigating through the undulating dunes and feeling the thrill of adventure.

After a day of excitement and exploration, retreat to the luxurious accommodations at Sealine Beach Resort. The resort offers a variety of lodging options, ranging from spacious villas to cozy chalets, ensuring a comfortable stay for every guest. The rooms and suites are tastefully designed, providing a blend of modern comforts and a touch of Arabian elegance. Whether you choose a room with a view of the azure waters or one nestled amidst the dunes, each accommodation option offers a tranquil sanctuary where you can unwind and rejuvenate.

When it comes to dining, Sealine Beach Resort spoils guests with a variety of options. From casual beachside cafes serving refreshing drinks and light bites to elegant restaurants offering a delectable array of international and local cuisines, there's something to satisfy every palate. Indulge in a romantic candlelit dinner by the sea, savoring fresh seafood dishes expertly prepared by the resort's talented chefs. Or opt for a casual al fresco lunch, basking in the warmth of the sun as you enjoy a sumptuous meal with your loved ones.

Sealine Beach Resort is more than just a place to stay; it's an experience that encompasses the beauty of Qatar's eastern coast and the world-class hospitality that the country is renowned for. Whether you're seeking relaxation, adventure, or simply a serene beach getaway, Sealine Beach Resort promises an unforgettable experience. Immerse yourself in the natural wonders of the Arabian Gulf, feel the sand between your toes, and let the cares of the world drift away as you embrace the magic of this coastal paradise.

Mangrove Forests: A Biodiverse Sanctuary in Al Thakira

Nestled along Qatar's northeastern coast, the Mangrove Forests of Al Thakira offer a unique and captivating natural sanctuary. These biodiverse ecosystems, consisting of dense mangrove trees and intricate water channels, provide a haven for various plant and animal species, making it a must-visit destination for nature enthusiasts and eco-conscious travelers.

The mangroves in Al Thakira serve as a vital breeding ground and nesting site for numerous migratory birds, including flamingos, herons, and egrets. These graceful creatures find solace and nourishment within the dense mangrove canopies and shallow waters of the forest. Visitors to the area are privileged to witness the magnificent sight of flocks of birds soaring through the sky or gracefully wading in the calm waters. The opportunity to observe and photograph these avian species in their natural habitat is truly awe-inspiring and offers a chance to witness their fascinating behaviors up close.

Exploring the mangroves can be done through guided kayaking or paddleboarding tours, allowing visitors to navigate through the narrow waterways, surrounded by towering mangrove trees. As the gentle current carries you through the channels, you'll find yourself immersed in a world of tranquility and natural beauty. The peaceful ambiance, interrupted only by the sounds of chirping birds and rustling leaves, creates a serene atmosphere that feels far removed from the bustling city life. Gliding silently through the mangroves, you'll have the opportunity to marvel at the intricate root systems of the trees, which form a labyrinth-like network and provide vital stability to the ecosystem.

The mangrove forests also play a significant role in maintaining the coastal ecosystem's balance. These incredible forests act as a natural filtration system, purifying the surrounding water and improving its quality. The roots of the mangroves trap sediments and filter out pollutants, making the water clearer and healthier. In addition to their water-purifying properties, mangroves serve as a crucial habitat for a variety of marine life. Fish, crabs, and mollusks find shelter and food among the mangrove roots, while juvenile species seek refuge in the protected and nutrient-rich environment. Snorkeling or participating in guided ecotours in the area allows visitors to witness the vibrant underwater world that thrives within and around the mangroves, providing an opportunity to observe the interconnectedness of the marine ecosystem.

Al Thakira's mangrove forests offer more than just a visual spectacle. They contribute to environmental conservation efforts and promote awareness about the importance of preserving natural habitats. Environmental organizations and local authorities work hand in hand to protect and restore these vital ecosystems. Educational programs and workshops are conducted to highlight the significance of mangrove ecosystems and the need for their conservation. Visitors have the opportunity to participate in these programs, gaining insights into the intricate web of life that depends on the mangroves and understanding the delicate balance between human activities and the environment.

A visit to the Mangrove Forests of Al Thakira not only provides an opportunity to appreciate the beauty of Qatar's natural landscapes but also fosters a deeper understanding of the importance of biodiversity and conservation. It is a place where visitors can connect with nature, immerse themselves in its wonders, and leave with a renewed appreciation for the Earth's remarkable biodiversity. The tranquility and serenity offered by the mangroves create a sense of harmony and connection with the natural world, reminding us of the need to protect and preserve these invaluable ecosystems for generations to come.

The Inland Sea: A Desert Gem of Tranquility

Deep within the expansive desert of Qatar lies a hidden gem, an extraordinary natural wonder known as the Inland Sea or Khor Al Udeid. This majestic expanse of turquoise water offers a unique outdoor adventure and a glimpse into the untouched beauty of Qatar's landscape. Accessible only by 4x4 vehicles, reaching this remote destination is an adventure in itself as visitors navigate through the undulating dunes.

As visitors approach the Inland Sea, they are greeted by a breathtaking contrast between the vast desert and the tranquil waters. The pristine saltwater inlet is surrounded by towering sand dunes, creating a mesmerizing landscape that captivates the senses. The silence and serenity enveloping the area create an atmosphere of tranquility, providing a welcome escape from the hustle and bustle of city life.

Upon arrival at the Inland Sea, visitors are immersed in a serene and tranquil environment. The beach, with its soft sands and gentle waves, offers a perfect setting for relaxation, picnics, and sunbathing. As the sun's rays glisten on the crystal-clear sea, it invites swimmers and water sports enthusiasts to immerse themselves in its inviting embrace. Whether it's floating lazily on the surface or diving beneath the shimmering waters, the

Inland Sea offers a refreshing respite from the desert heat.

Beyond its picturesque landscapes, the Inland Sea is also an ecosystem that supports a diverse range of wildlife. The surrounding desert is home to numerous desert-dwelling species, including the magnificent Arabian oryx and the graceful sand gazelle. These resilient creatures have adapted to the harsh desert environment and can be spotted gracefully moving across the golden sands. Birdwatchers will also find delight in observing various migratory and resident bird species that frequent the area, adding a touch of avian beauty to the natural tapestry.

For those seeking adrenaline-fueled experiences, the Inland Sea offers thrilling activities that embrace the spirit of adventure. Sandboarding, a popular pastime, involves riding down the steep slopes of the towering dunes on a specialized board, creating an exhilarating rush of adrenaline. The feeling of gliding down the silky sands, with the wind in your hair and the vast desert as your backdrop, is an unforgettable experience that will ignite your sense of adventure.

Another thrilling activity that draws visitors to the Inland Sea is dune bashing. Embarking on a heart-pounding off-road drive through the undulating dunes is a thrill-seeker's dream. Experienced drivers navigate the challenging terrain, maneuvering through the sandy peaks and valleys with precision. As the vehicle conquers the ever-shifting sands, passengers are treated to a rollercoaster-like experience that leaves them with a sense of awe and excitement.

Visiting the Inland Sea provides a unique opportunity to witness the raw beauty of Qatar's desert landscape and immerse oneself in the tranquility of nature. It's a place where the vastness of the desert meets the serenity of the sea, offering an unforgettable outdoor adventure for nature lovers and thrill-seekers alike. Whether you choose to relax on the beach, explore the diverse wildlife, or partake in adrenaline-pumping activities, the Inland Sea will leave an indelible mark on your heart and soul.

As you stand amidst the towering sand dunes, gazing out at the tranquil waters, you can't help but be in awe of the incredible beauty that surrounds you. The Inland Sea is a testament to the raw power and timeless allure of nature. It serves as a reminder that even in the most arid landscapes, life thrives and surprises await those who venture off the beaten path.

A journey to the Inland Sea is not just a physical adventure but a spiritual one as well. It is a place where you can disconnect from the noise of the world and reconnect with the natural rhythms of the earth. The vastness of the desert and the serenity of the sea create a harmonious symphony that soothes the soul and invigorates the spirit.

Whether you choose to embark on a thrilling sandboarding adventure, observe the desert's resilient wildlife, or simply bask in the tranquility of the beach, the Inland Sea promises an experience that is both awe-inspiring and humbling. It is a place where you can find solace in the vastness of the desert and discover the true essence of Qatar's natural wonders.

So, pack your bags, strap yourself into a 4x4 vehicle, and prepare to be captivated by the beauty of the Inland Sea. Let its untouched landscapes and breathtaking vistas transport you to a realm where time stands still, and the wonders of nature unfold before your eyes. The Inland Sea awaits, ready to enchant and inspire you with its untamed allure.

Zekreet: Where Art Meets Nature

Tucked away on Qatar's northwestern coast, Zekreet is a captivating destination that seamlessly blends natural beauty with artistic creations. This off-the-beaten-path location offers a unique outdoor experience where visitors can explore stunning rock formations, expansive beaches, and contemporary art installations.

One of the highlights of Zekreet is the mysterious rock formations known as the Zekreet Peninsula or the Film City. These natural sculptures, sculpted by wind and time, create a surreal and otherworldly atmosphere that has attracted filmmakers and photographers from around the world. As you venture into the Zekreet Peninsula, you'll be greeted by a landscape that seems to belong to another realm. The peculiar shapes and textures of the rocks make for a fascinating exploration and a photographer's paradise. The intricate formations seem to defy gravity, with arches, pillars, and valleys that showcase the artistry of nature. Walking through this geological wonderland, you'll feel a sense of awe and wonder as you witness the forces of nature at work.

Zekreet is also home to a significant art installation called "East-West/West-East" by renowned artist Richard Serra. This monumental sculpture consists of four steel plates placed in the middle of the desert, forming a corridor that stretches across the barren landscape. The massive steel structures stand in stark contrast to the surrounding desert, creating a visual spectacle that merges art and nature in an unexpected way. As you walk through the corridor, you'll experience a profound sense of scale and perspective, with the towering plates guiding your journey through the vastness of the landscape. The juxtaposition of the industrial materials against the natural backdrop creates a captivating artistic experience that challenges perceptions and ignites contemplation.

While Zekreet's rock formations and art installations are captivating, the coastal area of Zekreet boasts pristine beaches that are equally enchanting. The soft sands stretch for miles, inviting visitors to stroll along the shore, feel the warmth of the sun on their skin, and listen to the gentle lapping of the waves. The clear waters of the Arabian Gulf offer a refreshing respite, perfect for swimming, snorkeling, or simply floating on the calm surface. As you immerse yourself in the tranquility of the beach, you'll find a sense of serenity and relaxation that allows you to disconnect from the outside world and embrace the beauty of nature.

For those with a love for wildlife and natural landscapes, Zekreet offers access to the nearby Ras Abrouq Reserve. This protected area is known for its diverse ecosystem, with a variety of bird species, gazelles, and other desert-dwelling animals calling it home. The reserve is a haven for nature enthusiasts, offering opportunities for birdwatching, wildlife spotting, and hiking. As you explore the reserve's hiking trails, you'll be surrounded by breathtaking vistas of the coastline and the vast expanse of the desert. The panoramic views and the untouched beauty of Ras Abrouq Reserve will leave you in awe of Qatar's natural treasures.

Zekreet offers a unique combination of natural wonders and artistic expression, making it an intriguing destination for those seeking outdoor adventure and cultural exploration. It's a place where the lines between art and nature blur, leaving visitors captivated by the beauty that emerges from this harmonious union. Whether you're marveling at the mysterious rock formations, contemplating the monumental art installations, basking in the serenity of the beaches, or exploring the diverse wildlife of the nearby reserve, Zekreet promises a transformative experience that celebrates the majesty of nature and the power of artistic expression.

Modern Marvels and Futuristic Doha

In the ever-evolving landscape of Doha, several modern marvels and futuristic developments have taken shape, showcasing Qatar's vision for innovation, sustainability, and architectural grandeur. Explore these awe-inspiring destinations that embody the essence of a futuristic Doha.

Education City: A Hub for Cutting-Edge Learning and Innovation

Located on the outskirts of Doha, Education City stands as a remarkable testament to Qatar's unwavering commitment to education, research, and intellectual advancement. Spanning over 14 square kilometers, this visionary project brings together renowned universities, research institutions, and educational centers from around the world, creating a dynamic hub of knowledge and innovation.

At the heart of Education City's educational ecosystem are the satellite campuses of prestigious institutions, including Carnegie Mellon University, Georgetown University, and Texas A&M University. These esteemed universities offer a diverse range of academic programs, attracting students from across the globe to pursue higher education in Qatar. The campus architecture blends modern designs with traditional Qatari elements, creating an inspiring and conducive environment for learning and academic pursuits.

Education City is not just limited to classroom education; it also encompasses cutting-edge research facilities that propel Qatar's innovation landscape forward. The Qatar Science and Technology Park, located within Education City, serves as a thriving innovation hub that fosters collaboration between academia, industry, and startups. This collaborative environment drives research and development in various fields such as energy, information technology, and healthcare, pushing the boundaries of knowledge and technological advancements.

Visitors to Education City are in for a treat as they delve into its vibrant cultural scene. The Qatar National Library, an architectural masterpiece in its own right, serves as a beacon of learning and a hub for intellectual exchange. Housing an extensive collection of books, manuscripts, and digital resources, the library provides a platform for researchers, scholars, and book enthusiasts to explore a vast realm of knowledge.

Adjacent to the library, the Museum of Islamic Art Park invites visitors to immerse themselves in a world of artistic marvels. The park's beautifully landscaped grounds, dotted with sculptures and installations, offer a serene escape where art and nature converge. It is an ideal spot for leisurely strolls and quiet contemplation.

For those seeking outdoor recreational activities, Oxygen Park provides a refreshing retreat within Education City. This expansive park features lush green spaces, running and cycling tracks, and fitness zones, encouraging an active and healthy lifestyle. With its well-designed spaces and tranquil ambiance, Oxygen Park offers a much-needed respite for students, faculty, and visitors alike.

Education City stands out not only for its academic and research endeavors but also for its commitment to promoting a rich cultural experience. The integration of knowledge, innovation, and culture is evident in the various events, exhibitions, and festivals hosted within its premises. From captivating art exhibitions to thought-provoking lectures and workshops, Education City fosters a vibrant intellectual and cultural atmosphere that stimulates the mind and nurtures creativity.

Moreover, Education City's commitment to sustainability is evident in its eco-friendly practices and initiatives. The buildings within the campus incorporate sustainable design principles, utilizing energy-efficient systems and materials. The integration of green spaces and landscaping contributes to a more environmentally friendly and aesthetically pleasing environment.

Education City serves as a beacon of Qatar's vision for the future, where education, innovation, and culture intertwine harmoniously. It represents a significant investment in human capital, as well as the country's dedication to fostering a knowledge-based economy. By bringing together world-class institutions, cutting-edge research facilities, and cultural attractions, Education City offers a comprehensive and immersive experience for visitors seeking to witness the future of learning and intellectual pursuits.

Visiting Education City is not only an opportunity to explore the forefront of education and research but also a chance to engage with a vibrant community of scholars, students, and intellectuals from diverse backgrounds. Whether you are a student aspiring to pursue higher education, a researcher looking for collaborative opportunities, or simply a curious traveler with a thirst for knowledge, Education City provides an enriching and inspiring experience that encapsulates the essence of Qatar's commitment to intellectual growth and innovation.

Lusail City: Qatar's Futuristic Urban Development Project

Nestled along the picturesque coast of Qatar, Lusail City is an ambitious and visionary urban development project that embodies the nation's commitment to sustainability, innovation, and quality of life. Envisioned as a smart city and a blueprint for urban living, Lusail City is poised to become a self-sustaining and environmentally conscious community that seamlessly blends cutting-edge technology, entertainment, and the well-being of its residents.

At the heart of Lusail City lies the magnificent Lusail Iconic Stadium, which will serve as the centerpiece for the opening and closing ceremonies of the FIFA World Cup 2022. Designed to showcase Qatar's commitment to sustainability, the stadium's architecture incorporates energy-efficient features, state-of-the-art technology, and a striking aesthetic appeal. The stadium's innovative design ensures optimal comfort for spectators while minimizing its environmental impact.

Beyond the grandeur of the Lusail Iconic Stadium, Lusail City encompasses a diverse range of residential, commercial, and entertainment districts, each offering unique experiences and amenities. The Marina District, with its scenic waterfront setting, provides residents and visitors alike with a luxurious and serene lifestyle. This district features upscale residences, elegant shopping promenades, world-class marinas, and a vibrant atmosphere that seamlessly blends relaxation and entertainment.

The entertainment district of Lusail City is a captivating hub of excitement, promising an array of attractions and activities for all ages. Lusail Entertainment City is a focal point of this district, offering theme parks, shopping malls, entertainment venues, and leisure spaces where families and friends can gather to create lasting memories. From thrilling rides and immersive experiences to fine dining and cultural performances, the entertainment district of Lusail City is a captivating destination for leisure and recreation.

Lusail City places great emphasis on promoting a healthy and active lifestyle for its residents and visitors. The city boasts an extensive network of parks, cycling tracks, and pedestrian-friendly spaces, encouraging outdoor activities and fostering a sense of well-being. Residents can enjoy leisurely strolls along beautifully landscaped promenades, engage in various sports activities, or simply relax in the tranquil green spaces that dot the cityscape. The incorporation of nature and greenery into the urban fabric of Lusail City enhances the overall aesthetic appeal and contributes to a sustainable environment.

A defining feature of Lusail City is its smart infrastructure, which leverages cutting-edge technology to enhance the quality of life for its inhabitants. The city's intelligent transportation systems optimize traffic flow, reduce congestion, and provide efficient connectivity. Smart energy management systems ensure the responsible use of resources, minimizing waste and maximizing efficiency. Lusail City also prioritizes connectivity, offering seamless integration of digital services, high-speed internet access, and advanced communication networks. The integration of technology throughout the city not only enhances convenience but also reduces the ecological footprint, aligning with Lusail City's commitment to sustainability.

The vision for Lusail City extends beyond mere urban development. It strives to create a vibrant and inclusive community that fosters social cohesion and a sense of belonging. The city's design prioritizes public spaces, community centers, and cultural venues, encouraging social interactions and community engagement. Lusail City aims to cultivate a rich and diverse social fabric, where residents can connect, collaborate, and celebrate the vibrant tapestry of cultures that make up Qatar.

Qanat Quartier: Mediterranean-Inspired Living on The Pearl-Qatar

Nestled within the iconic man-made island of The Pearl-Qatar, Qanat Quartier is a vibrant residential district that transports its residents and visitors to the charm and ambiance of a Mediterranean coastal town. With its inspired design and unique living experience, Qanat Quartier stands as a testament to Doha's commitment to creating futuristic and culturally immersive developments.

Qanat Quartier takes its inspiration from the intricate canal system of Venice, Italy. As you step into this waterfront community, you are immediately greeted by a picturesque scene of canals winding through the district, reminiscent of the Venetian waterways. The network of canals adds a touch of enchantment and provides a distinct character to the neighborhood.

One of the highlights of Qanat Quartier is its remarkable architecture that draws from Mediterranean influences. The buildings showcase the beauty of Venetian-style bridges that gracefully arch over the canals, connecting various parts of the district. These bridges not only serve as functional crossings but also contribute to the overall aesthetic appeal, creating a sense of romance and elegance.

The enchanting piazzas of Qanat Quartier further enhance its Mediterranean atmosphere. These lively squares are adorned with charming cafes, boutique shops, and restaurants, inviting residents and visitors to indulge in a leisurely stroll, shop for unique treasures, and savor delectable cuisine. The piazzas serve as vibrant gathering spots, fostering a sense of community and providing opportunities for social interaction.

Qanat Quartier offers an array of residential options, catering to diverse preferences and lifestyles. Stylish apartments and spacious townhouses are nestled within the district, each exuding its own character and charm. The architecture seamlessly blends traditional Mediterranean elements with modern designs, creating residences that are as visually appealing as they are comfortable.

Living in Qanat Quartier provides residents with more than just beautiful homes; it offers a tranquil and scenic lifestyle. The district's strategic location on The Pearl-Qatar grants residents easy access to the azure waters of the Arabian Gulf. Pristine beaches are just a stone's throw away, allowing residents to relax, unwind, and enjoy breathtaking views of the ocean.

The presence of the canals adds a touch of serenity and tranquility to everyday life in Qanat Quartier. The gentle flow of water and the picturesque bridges create an atmosphere of calmness, making it an idyllic setting for residents to find respite from the bustling city. Whether it's a morning walk along the canals or a peaceful evening spent on a gondola ride, Qanat Quartier provides a soothing retreat within the heart of Doha.

Beyond its residential allure, Qanat Quartier is also home to a vibrant array of amenities and facilities. The district features a variety of retail outlets, from upscale boutiques to quaint shops, offering residents and visitors a diverse shopping experience. Additionally, the charming cafes and restaurants lining the promenades provide opportunities to indulge in culinary delights, whether it's enjoying a cup of coffee with a view or savoring a delicious meal in a picturesque setting.

Qanat Quartier seamlessly combines the beauty of architecture, the tranquility of canals, and the vibrant atmosphere of a Mediterranean town. It captures the essence of a waterfront community, allowing residents to experience a unique and captivating way of living. The careful attention to detail and the integration of natural elements make Qanat Quartier a truly extraordinary destination within Doha.

As the sun sets over the glistening waters of the Arabian Gulf, Qanat Quartier takes on a magical ambiance. The reflection of lights on the canals creates a mesmerizing spectacle, adding to the allure and allure of this futuristic residential district. Qanat Quartier stands as a testament to Doha's commitment to creating innovative and culturally immersive developments that push the boundaries of architectural excellence and offer residents a truly exceptional living experience.

Msheireb Downtown Doha: A Sustainable Smart City

Msheireb Downtown Doha is an ambitious urban regeneration project that has transformed the oldest district of Doha into a sustainable smart city. With a vision to preserve Qatari heritage while incorporating cutting-edge technology and sustainable practices, this development stands as a shining example of sustainable urban living.

The project was initiated by Msheireb Properties, a leading real estate development company in Qatar, with the aim of revitalizing the historic heart of Doha. The district, once a vibrant commercial and residential area, had experienced neglect over the years. However, with the launch of Msheireb Downtown Doha, a new chapter in the district's history began.

One of the key principles driving the development of Msheireb Downtown Doha is sustainability. The district showcases energy-efficient buildings, smart infrastructure, and advanced sustainability features that have earned it numerous accolades and certifications, including LEED (Leadership in Energy and Environmental Design) Platinum certification.

The architectural design of Msheireb Downtown Doha seamlessly blends traditional Qatari architecture with contemporary elements. The buildings draw inspiration from Qatari heritage, incorporating elements such as wind towers and Mashrabiya screens, while also embracing modern materials and technologies. This harmonious blend of old and new creates a unique visual identity for the district.

A significant aspect of Msheireb Downtown Doha is its focus on cultural preservation. The district is home to the Msheireb Museums, a collection of restored heritage houses that provide insights into Qatar's history and heritage. These museums showcase various aspects of

Qatari life, including architecture, traditions, and community development. Through interactive exhibits and immersive experiences, visitors can delve into the rich cultural tapestry of Qatar and gain a deeper understanding of its evolution over the years.

Beyond its cultural attractions, Msheireb Downtown Doha offers a vibrant mix of upscale retail and dining establishments. The district is dotted with boutique shops, designer stores, and gourmet restaurants, providing residents and visitors with a diverse range of shopping and culinary experiences, the district caters to discerning tastes and preferences.

One of the defining features of Msheireb Downtown Doha is its pedestrian-friendly design and vibrant public spaces. The district boasts wide, shaded walkways, landscaped parks, and inviting squares where people can gather, socialize, and enjoy the outdoors. This emphasis on creating walkable spaces encourages a sense of community and promotes a healthier and more sustainable lifestyle.

Msheireb Downtown Doha goes beyond just buildings and infrastructure; it is a holistic approach to urban living. The district incorporates smart technologies and innovative solutions to enhance the quality of life for its residents and visitors. From smart waste management systems to energy-efficient lighting, the district embraces the concept of a smart city, where technology is harnessed to optimize resources and improve sustainability.

Residents of Msheireb Downtown Doha enjoy a host of amenities and services that cater to their needs. The district offers a range of residential options, from apartments to townhouses, designed to meet modern living standards while maintaining a strong connection to Qatari heritage. Residents also have access to educational institutions, healthcare facilities, and recreational spaces, ensuring a comprehensive and fulfilling lifestyle within the district.

Furthermore, Msheireb Downtown Doha promotes sustainable transportation options, with a focus on reducing reliance on private vehicles. The district integrates an efficient public transportation network, including tram systems and buses, making it easy for residents and visitors to navigate the area without the need for cars. This approach reduces congestion, lowers carbon emissions, and contributes to a greener and more sustainable environment.

In conclusion, Msheireb Downtown Doha stands as a testament to the successful transformation of a historic district into a sustainable smart city. The project showcases the harmonious blend of Qatari heritage and modern innovation, offering a glimpse into the future of urban living. With its energy-efficient buildings, smart infrastructure, cultural attractions, and pedestrian-friendly design, the district exemplifies the possibilities of sustainable development while preserving the essence of Qatar's rich heritage. Msheireb Downtown Doha sets a benchmark for sustainable urban regeneration projects worldwide, inspiring other cities to embrace sustainability, cultural preservation, and technological advancements in their urban planning endeavors.

Aspire Zone: Sports and Recreation Excellence

Aspire Zone, also known as Doha Sports City, is a testament to Doha's unwavering commitment to sports and recreation excellence. Spanning an expansive area, this world-class sports complex offers state-of-the-art facilities for a wide range of sports, making it a hub for athletes, sports enthusiasts, and visitors seeking active and healthy experiences.

At the heart of Aspire Zone stands the iconic Aspire Tower, a striking skyscraper that serves as a symbol of Qatar's sporting aspirations. This architectural marvel reaches a height of 300 meters, dominating the Doha skyline. The tower's sleek design and illuminated exterior make it a captivating sight, especially when lit up during special events and celebrations.

One of the highlights of the Aspire Tower is its revolving restaurant, located at the top. This unique dining experience allows guests to indulge in exquisite cuisine while enjoying panoramic views of Doha from a breathtaking vantage point. Aspire Tower's restaurant has become a popular destination for locals and tourists alike, combining fine dining with unparalleled vistas of the city.

Adjacent to the tower is the Aspire Dome, one of the largest indoor multipurpose sports venues in the world. This impressive structure encompasses a vast space that can accommodate a range of sports, including football, basketball, volleyball, handball, and more. Its versatile design allows for the hosting of international tournaments, sporting events, and training sessions across various disciplines.

The Aspire Dome has state-of-the-art facilities, including training halls, fitness centers, and physiotherapy clinics, catering to the needs of athletes and sports teams. With its climate-controlled environment, it provides a comfortable and optimal setting for training and competitions, regardless of the external weather conditions. The dome has witnessed the participation of renowned sports teams, the staging of international championships, and the development of emerging talents in various disciplines.

Complementing the sports venues, Aspire Zone is also home to the expansive Aspire Park. This lush green space spans over 88 hectares and offers a serene and picturesque environment for outdoor activities, relaxation, and recreation. The park features meticulously landscaped gardens, walking and jogging trails, playgrounds, and picnic areas, providing visitors with a tranquil escape from the bustling city.

Aspire Park's scenic beauty and well-maintained facilities attract families, fitness enthusiasts, and nature lovers. It serves as a haven for outdoor enthusiasts, who can engage in activities such as cycling, rollerblading, yoga, or simply enjoying a leisurely stroll amidst the park's natural splendor. The park's serene ambiance, coupled with its proximity to the Aspire Zone sports facilities, creates a seamless integration of nature and sports, encouraging a balanced and healthy lifestyle.

In addition to the primary attractions, Aspire Zone hosts various sports academies, training centers, and sports-related organizations. These institutions provide professional coaching, training programs, and development opportunities for athletes of all ages and skill levels. The dedication to nurturing talent and promoting sports excellence is evident in the comprehensive sports infrastructure and support system within Aspire Zone.

Aspire Zone has gained international recognition for its commitment to sustainable practices. The complex incorporates environmentally friendly initiatives, including energy-efficient lighting systems, waste management programs, and the use of recycled materials. These sustainable efforts align with Qatar's broader sustainability goals and demonstrate Doha's dedication to responsible development.

Moreover, Aspire Zone has been instrumental in fostering a sports culture and encouraging active participation within the local community. It regularly organizes sporting events, tournaments, and community-driven initiatives to engage residents and inspire a passion for sports. These endeavors contribute to the overall well-being and social fabric of Doha, promoting inclusivity, teamwork, and the pursuit of personal excellence.

Aspire Zone's impact extends beyond the sports arena. It serves as a catalyst for economic growth, attracting international sports organizations, sponsors, and visitors to Doha. The influx of sports-related tourism and events generates significant revenue, strengthens Qatar's position as a global sporting destination, and enhances the country's overall reputation in the international sporting community.

Hamad International Airport: The Gateway to the Future

Hamad International Airport (HIA) is not just an aviation hub; it is a testament to Doha's unwavering commitment to innovation, luxury, and providing an exceptional passenger experience. Designed to accommodate the ever-growing number of travelers, HIA has redefined the concept of airports with its cutting-edge technology, striking architecture, and world-class amenities.

As soon as passengers step foot into HIA, they are enveloped by an atmosphere of elegance and grandeur. The airport boasts a plethora of modern facilities that cater to the desires of discerning travelers. Designer boutiques featuring renowned brands line the corridors, offering a luxury shopping experience like no other. From high-end fashion labels to exquisite jewelry and accessories, these boutiques provide a haven for fashion enthusiasts and connoisseurs.

HIA's premium lounges redefine the concept of comfort and relaxation. The lounges offer an oasis of tranquility amidst the bustling airport, where travelers can unwind and rejuvenate before their flights. Equipped with luxurious furnishings, private suites, spa services, and gourmet dining options, these lounges provide an unparalleled level of pampering and exclusivity.

For gastronomic delights, HIA leaves no stone unturned. The airport is home to an array of fine dining options, ranging from international cuisines to local delicacies. Travelers can savor culinary masterpieces crafted by renowned chefs, allowing their taste buds to embark on a journey of flavors and gastronomic exploration.

What sets HIA apart is its commitment to celebrating Qatari culture and heritage. The airport showcases a curated collection of artwork and installations that pay homage to the nation's rich traditions and artistic heritage. From striking sculptures to vibrant murals, these artistic expressions create an immersive and visually captivating environment, reflecting Qatar's deep-rooted cultural identity.

HIA's passenger-centric approach is at the heart of its design. The airport seamlessly integrates advanced technology to streamline the travel experience, making it convenient and efficient for passengers. Self-check-in kiosks provide a hassle-free process, reducing wait times and allowing travelers to proceed smoothly through the airport. Automated immigration systems further expedite the entry process, ensuring a seamless transition for international visitors.

Smart boarding gates equipped with state-of-the-art technology enhance the boarding experience, providing real-time updates and facilitating a smooth embarkation process. Passengers can navigate the airport with ease, guided by digital signage and interactive information screens that offer intuitive directions and flight updates.

The iconic C-shaped terminal of HIA is a visual masterpiece, combining architectural splendor with functionality. The design not only provides a distinctive aesthetic appeal but also ensures efficiency in passenger flow and operational processes. The terminal's spaciousness and intuitive layout create a sense of openness and tranquility, allowing travelers to navigate comfortably.

The duty-free shopping area within HIA is an experience in itself. Spanning an expansive space, it offers a diverse range of products, from luxury goods to local souvenirs. Travelers can indulge in tax-free shopping and explore a vast selection of perfumes, cosmetics, electronics, and more. The duty-free shopping experience at HIA is an opportunity to discover exclusive products and take home cherished mementos of their journey.

Efficient transit facilities at HIA make it an ideal layover destination. The airport provides a range of services and amenities for passengers in transit, ensuring their comfort and entertainment during the interlude between flights. From relaxing in luxurious lounges to enjoying spa treatments or even exploring the airport's art installations, HIA offers a myriad of options to make transit a pleasurable experience.

Hamad International Airport is more than a mere transportation hub; it is a gateway to the future. Its innovative approach to design, focus on luxury and passenger experience, and incorporation of cutting-edge technology make it a shining example of what airports can aspire to be. From the moment passengers arrive until their departure, HIA aims to deliver an unforgettable and seamless travel experience, reflecting the vision and ambition of Doha as a city that embraces the future with open arms.

Qanat Quartier: European Elegance and Coastal Living on The Pearl-Qatar

Qanat Quartier, nestled within the iconic man-made island of The Pearl-Qatar, presents visitors with a mesmerizing blend of European elegance and coastal living. This vibrant residential district stands as a testament to Doha's innovative and forward-thinking approach to urban planning, creating an enchanting destination that transports visitors to a world of charm and sophistication.

Drawing inspiration from the intricate canal system of Venice, Qanat Quartier features picturesque canals, charming bridges, and captivating piazzas that emulate the ambiance of a Mediterranean coastal town. The district's architecture exudes a distinctive Venetian-style charm, characterized by colorful townhouses, inviting courtyards, and waterfront promenades.

A leisurely exploration of Qanat Quartier reveals a myriad of delights. Visitors can embark on gondola rides, gliding along the canals, taking in the scenic beauty and immersing themselves in the tranquil surroundings. The waterfront promenades invite leisurely strolls, with artisanal boutiques, stylish cafes, and delightful restaurants dotting the streets, offering a plethora of options for relaxation, shopping, and culinary indulgence.

The residential options in Qanat Quartier range from stylish apartments to spacious townhouses, each exuding its own unique charm. Residents enjoy a serene and scenic lifestyle, surrounded by the azure waters of the Arabian Gulf. The community provides a harmonious blend of comfort, privacy, and proximity to a range of amenities, ensuring a balanced and fulfilling living experience.

Qanat Quartier is not only a residential haven but also a vibrant destination for cultural immersion. Throughout the district, artistic elements and architectural details pay homage to Qatari heritage and culture. The infusion of Qatari motifs, traditional craftsmanship, and contemporary design creates a sense of place and identity, further enriching the overall experience.

As dusk descends, Qanat Quartier transforms into a magical setting. The enchanting lighting, coupled with the soothing sound of water gently flowing through the canals, creates an ambiance of serenity and romance. Residents and visitors can relish the Mediterranean-inspired atmosphere, savoring delectable cuisine al fresco or enjoying a leisurely evening by the waterfront, enveloped in a sense of tranquility and beauty.

Qanat Quartier stands as a testament to Doha's vision for creating communities that harmoniously blend innovation, aesthetics, and a high quality of life. Its European elegance and coastal living concept provide a unique and alluring experience for residents and visitors alike.

CHAPTER SIX

SHOPPING AND ENTERTAINMENT

Doha is a unique place where shopping and entertainment converge to create a captivating experience. Indulge in a world of luxury and culture as you explore the vibrant city's shopping and entertainment offerings.

Villaggio Mall: Retail Therapy and Family Fun Under One Roof

Located in the heart of Doha, Villaggio Mall stands as a testament to luxury, entertainment, and family-friendly attractions. As you step into this sprawling mall, you are instantly transported to an enchanting world designed in the style of an Italian village. The architectural marvel of Villaggio Mall features picturesque canals, charming bridges, and a stunning glass ceiling that mimics a clear blue sky, creating an atmosphere of elegance and sophistication.

For fashion enthusiasts, Villaggio Mall is a paradise that caters to all tastes and preferences. Boasting over 200 stores, the mall showcases a diverse range of international brands and high-end fashion labels. Whether you're in search of designer boutiques or popular retailers, you'll find a plethora of options to satisfy your fashion cravings. Explore the latest clothing trends, discover unique accessories, browse through exquisite cosmetics, indulge in cutting-edge electronics, or adorn your home with tasteful decor. Villaggio Mall ensures that every visitor can embark on a delightful retail therapy journey, finding something special to take home.

However, Villaggio Mall offers much more than just a shopping extravaganza. It is a destination where entertainment takes center stage, captivating visitors of all ages. At the heart of the mall lies Gondolania, an expansive indoor theme park that promises an exhilarating experience. Here, both kids and adults can immerse themselves in a world of adventure, where thrilling rides, arcade games, and go-karting await. The joyous laughter and excited screams fill the air as families create unforgettable memories together. Additionally, Gondolania boasts an ice rink, providing a cool and exciting escape for those who enjoy gliding on ice. Whether you're a seasoned skater or a beginner taking your first steps, the Gondolania Ice Rink offers a delightful experience that combines leisure and excitement.

Movie enthusiasts can find solace in Villaggio Mall's state-of-the-art cinema, where the latest blockbusters are screened in utmost comfort and style. Sit back, relax, and lose yourself in the magic of the silver screen as you immerse yourself in captivating stories brought to life with impeccable visuals and immersive sound. Villaggio

Mall ensures that entertainment is not limited to shopping alone, but extends to the realms of joy and imagination.

After a day of shopping and entertainment, Villaggio Mall presents an array of dining options to satisfy your taste buds. The mall's food court and restaurants offer a diverse culinary experience that caters to a variety of palates. Indulge in international cuisines that span the globe, from tantalizing Asian flavors to mouthwatering Mediterranean delights. Sample local delicacies and immerse yourself in the rich tapestry of Qatari cuisine. Whether you're seeking a quick bite on the go or a leisurely meal with loved ones, Villaggio Mall provides an exquisite selection of cafes, fast-food chains, and upscale dining establishments. Let your taste buds embark on a journey of flavors, and savor the culinary delights that await you.

Villaggio Mall is not merely a shopping center; it is a destination where luxury, entertainment, and culinary delights converge. It offers a unique experience where visitors can indulge in the finest retail therapy, immerse themselves in thrilling entertainment, and savor delectable flavors from around the world. The mall's commitment to providing a family-friendly environment ensures that everyone, from children to adults, can find something to captivate their hearts and create cherished memories. Whether you're strolling along the canals, enjoying the excitement of the theme park, losing yourself in the magic of cinema, or savoring the flavors of a sumptuous meal, Villaggio Mall invites you to experience a world of wonder, enchantment, and pure delight.

Doha Festival City: Shop, Dine, and Indulge in Entertainment Galore

As one of the largest shopping and entertainment destinations in Qatar, Doha Festival City offers an immersive experience that caters to visitors of all ages. This expansive complex is a must-visit destination for both locals and tourists, featuring a diverse mix of retail outlets, dining establishments, and entertainment venues.

Shop Till You Drop

Doha Festival City is a shopaholic's paradise, boasting an extensive selection of international and local brands. With a wide range of fashion, electronics, home decor, and lifestyle products, the mall caters to every shopper's preferences. From flagship stores of renowned luxury labels to specialty boutiques showcasing unique and trendy items, there is something to suit every style and budget. The spacious walkways and vibrant atmosphere create a delightful shopping experience, allowing visitors to explore and discover a multitude of options.

A Culinary Journey

Indulging in a culinary adventure at Doha Festival City is an absolute must for food enthusiasts. The mall boasts a diverse range of dining options that cater to various tastes and preferences, ensuring there is something to please every palate. From casual eateries serving quick bites to upscale restaurants providing a truly memorable dining experience, the culinary offerings at Doha Festival City are sure to tantalize your taste buds.

One of the highlights of the mall's dining scene is the opportunity to embark on a culinary journey around the world. The array of international cuisines available allows visitors to explore and savor flavors from different corners of the globe. Whether you have a craving for Middle Eastern delights, Asian fusion cuisine, European classics, or other culinary traditions, Doha Festival City has a plethora of choices to satisfy your appetite.

For those seeking a casual dining experience, the mall offers a wide selection of eateries serving quick bites and satisfying meals. Whether you're in the mood for a juicy burger, a comforting plate of pasta, or a flavorful Middle Eastern wrap, you'll find a range of options that deliver delicious flavors and convenient dining.

If you're looking to elevate your dining experience, Doha Festival City is home to upscale restaurants that promise an extraordinary culinary journey. These establishments provide an immersive and refined atmosphere, complemented by impeccable service and exceptional gastronomic creations. From sophisticated seafood delicacies to delectable steaks and international fusion creations, these upscale venues offer a dining experience that is as memorable as it is delicious.

Beyond the diverse range of cuisines available, Doha Festival City also caters to those seeking experimental gastronomic experiences. Some restaurants in the mall push the boundaries of traditional flavors and culinary techniques, offering innovative and avant-garde dishes. Whether you're a foodie with an adventurous palate or simply curious to try something new, these restaurants provide an opportunity to engage in a culinary adventure that surprises and delights.

In addition to the culinary offerings, Doha Festival City also features a vibrant and welcoming ambiance in its dining areas. The stylish and comfortable seating arrangements allow visitors to relax and enjoy their meals in a pleasant atmosphere. Whether you're dining with friends, family, or as a couple, the mall provides a variety of spaces suitable for different group sizes and occasions.

Moreover, the mall's commitment to quality extends beyond the food itself. The restaurants at Doha Festival City prioritize using fresh ingredients, and many establishments source local and sustainable produce, supporting the local community and promoting eco-conscious dining practices.

Entertainment Galore
Doha Festival City takes entertainment to the next level, ensuring visitors have a thrilling and enjoyable time. The mall is home to a state-of-the-art cinema complex, offering the latest movie releases in comfortable theaters

equipped with cutting-edge audiovisual technology. Movie buffs can catch their favorite films and immerse themselves in captivating storytelling.

For those seeking an adrenaline rush, the indoor theme park within Doha Festival City provides an exhilarating experience. The park features a range of thrilling rides and attractions that cater to both children and adults alike. From roller coasters to virtual reality experiences, visitors can enjoy a dose of excitement and adventure.

In addition to the cinema and theme park, Doha Festival City hosts a variety of events to keep visitors entertained and engaged. Live performances, including music concerts, dance shows, and theatrical productions, bring the mall to life with vibrant energy. Art exhibitions showcasing local and international talent add a touch of creativity and cultural appreciation. Visitors can also participate in interactive experiences, workshops, and demonstrations that engage and inspire.

The diverse range of entertainment options ensures that there is always something exciting happening at Doha Festival City. Whether you're a movie lover, a thrill-seeker, a culture enthusiast, or simply looking for a fun-filled day out, the mall offers an array of activities and events to suit every interest.

In conclusion, Doha Festival City stands out as a premier shopping and entertainment destination in Qatar. With its vast selection of retail outlets, diverse dining options, state-of-the-art cinema complex, thrilling indoor theme park, and engaging events, the mall provides a comprehensive experience that caters to the needs and desires of visitors from all walks of life. Overall, Doha Festival City promises an unforgettable experience that captures the essence of retail therapy and entertainment galore.

Nightlife in Doha: Vibrant Bars, Clubs, and Cultural Performances

As the sun sets in Doha, the city transforms into a vibrant playground for those seeking an exhilarating nightlife experience. With its diverse range of options, Doha offers a dynamic and energetic atmosphere that caters to a wide array of tastes and preferences. Whether you're in the mood for a trendy bar, a pulsating nightclub, or captivating cultural performances, the city has something for everyone.

Doha's nightlife is renowned for its vibrant bars and clubs that dot the cityscape, providing a haven for those seeking entertainment and socializing after dark. The city boasts a growing number of establishments that cater to different tastes and preferences, ensuring that there is a perfect venue for every visitor. Whether you're looking for a laid-back rooftop lounge with breathtaking views of the city skyline or a bustling nightclub with live music and DJ performances, Doha's nightlife scene has it all. These venues often offer carefully crafted cocktails, showcasing the artistry of skilled mixologists who blend flavors and ingredients to create unique and unforgettable drinks. Sip on your favorite concoction while enjoying the ambience and mingling with locals and expats who frequent these popular establishments.

For those interested in immersing themselves in Doha's rich cultural heritage, the city's nightlife scene also offers captivating cultural performances. Doha takes immense pride in its traditions and is eager to share its cultural treasures with visitors. Throughout the city, various venues host enchanting performances that showcase traditional music, dance, and theatrical arts. From mesmerizing Qatari folk dances that tell stories of the nation's heritage to soul-stirring performances of Arabian music, these cultural showcases provide an immersive experience for all who attend. Local artists and performers demonstrate their talents, offering a glimpse into the beauty and depth of Qatari culture. The rich melodies, vibrant costumes, and intricate choreography create a sensory journey that transports the audience to a world of enchantment. Attending one of these cultural performances is not only a form of entertainment but also an opportunity to gain a deeper understanding and appreciation for the local traditions and artistic expressions.

Doha's nightlife is not limited to bars, clubs, and cultural performances; it also embraces eventful evenings that offer an extra layer of excitement and entertainment. The city's dynamic nightlife scene often features special events and themed nights that cater to specific interests and preferences. Whether it's a themed party where guests dress up in extravagant costumes, a live concert featuring local or international artists, or an evening of laughter at a comedy show, Doha ensures that there is always something happening to entertain and engage night owls. These events provide a platform for both established and emerging talents to showcase their skills and captivate audiences. Open mic nights, for example, offer a chance for aspiring musicians, poets, and performers to take the stage and share their artistry with a supportive crowd. To make the most of your nights out in Doha, it's advisable to keep an eye on event listings and local recommendations, ensuring that you don't miss out on the latest happenings and exciting opportunities to create lasting memories.

Doha's nightlife scene is a reflection of the city's dynamism and its people's love for celebration, entertainment, and socializing. Whether you choose to unwind at a stylish bar, dance the night away in a lively club, immerse yourself in cultural performances, or attend special events, the energy and liveliness of Doha's nightlife are sure to leave a lasting impression. With its diverse range of options and the warm hospitality of its people, Doha offers an unparalleled nightlife experience that combines entertainment, cultural immersion, and the opportunity to connect with locals and fellow visitors from around the world. So, as the sun sets on the horizon, venture out into the vibrant nightlife of Doha and let the city's energetic atmosphere embrace you in its embrace.

The Gate Mall: Luxury Shopping and Artistic Flair

Situated in the prestigious West Bay area of Doha, The Gate Mall stands as a beacon of sophistication and elegance, offering visitors a truly upscale and refined shopping experience. With its boutique-style design, the mall exudes a sense of exclusivity and tastefulness, attracting discerning shoppers from near and far. From its carefully curated selection of renowned international brands to its luxurious fashion labels and exclusive designer boutiques, The Gate Mall sets a new standard for high-end shopping in Doha.

As you enter The Gate Mall, you are immediately captivated by its elegant ambiance and stylish architecture. The interiors are meticulously designed with a harmonious blend of contemporary aesthetics and classic elements. From the gleaming marble floors to the ornate chandeliers that illuminate the hallways, every detail has been carefully chosen to create an atmosphere of luxury and refinement.

The shopping experience at The Gate Mall is unparalleled. The mall boasts a curated selection of prestigious international brands, including renowned fashion houses, jewelry designers, and luxury lifestyle labels. From haute couture to ready-to-wear collections, visitors can explore the latest trends and indulge in the world of high fashion. The exclusive designer boutiques offer a personalized and intimate shopping experience, where dedicated staff cater to the individual needs and desires of each customer.

In addition to its exquisite shopping offerings, The Gate Mall goes beyond the realm of retail to embrace the world of art. Throughout the mall, you'll find captivating art installations and galleries that add a cultural touch to the overall experience. These artistic elements not only elevate the aesthetic appeal of the mall but also create a sense of immersion and inspiration for visitors. From contemporary sculptures to thought-provoking paintings, the art displays at The Gate Mall showcase the creativity and talent of both local and international artists.

One of the highlights of The Gate Mall is its art galleries, which provide a platform for emerging artists to showcase their works and for art enthusiasts to discover new talents. These galleries host regular exhibitions featuring a diverse range of artistic styles and mediums, including paintings, photography, sculpture, and mixed media. Whether you're an avid art collector or simply appreciate the beauty of visual expressions, the art galleries at The Gate Mall offer a captivating journey through the world of contemporary art.

Beyond the shopping and art, The Gate Mall also offers a selection of sophisticated dining options to cater to the discerning palates of its visitors. From chic cafes to gourmet restaurants, the culinary offerings at the mall are as refined as the shopping experience itself. Whether you're in the mood for a leisurely brunch, a sumptuous dinner, or a delightful afternoon tea, the dining venues at The Gate Mall provide a perfect blend of delectable cuisine, elegant ambiance, and impeccable service.

The Gate Mall is not just a destination for shopping and dining; it's a place where luxury and culture converge. The mall regularly hosts a range of events and activities that add vibrancy and entertainment to the visitor experience. These events may include fashion shows, live performances, art workshops, and cultural celebrations, providing a dynamic and engaging atmosphere for shoppers and art enthusiasts alike.

Convenience is also paramount at The Gate Mall, as it offers ample parking facilities and easy accessibility from various parts of the city. Its location in the prestigious West Bay area makes it a desirable destination for both locals and international visitors who seek an exclusive and refined shopping experience.

CHAPTER SEVEN

PRACTICAL TIPS AND RECOMMENDATIONS

As you navigate through the heart of the Arabian Gulf, here are some practical tips and recommendations to ensure a memorable visit.

Accommodation Options: From Luxurious Hotels to Budget-Friendly Stays

When it comes to accommodations in Doha, you'll find a wide range of options to suit every budget and preference. Here are some recommendations:

Luxury Hotels

Doha is renowned for its opulent accommodations that cater to the discerning traveler seeking an extraordinary stay. The city boasts a collection of world-class luxury hotels that epitomize elegance, offer exceptional amenities, breathtaking views, and provide unparalleled service. When indulging in the lap of luxury is your desire, consider the following iconic establishments:

The St. Regis Doha: Situated on the shores of the Arabian Gulf, The St. Regis Doha presents a lavish retreat with its palatial rooms and suites adorned with contemporary Arabian-inspired decor. Immerse yourself in the epitome of luxury as you enjoy exclusive dining experiences, rejuvenating spa treatments, and the legendary St. Regis Butler Service.

Four Seasons Hotel Doha: Nestled in the heart of the city, Four Seasons Hotel Doha exudes sophistication and grandeur. Each guest room and suite boasts stunning views of the sparkling Gulf waters or the city skyline. With its impressive array of dining options, luxurious spa, and world-class facilities, this hotel ensures an unforgettable stay.

Marsa Malaz Kempinski: Located on its own island, Marsa Malaz Kempinski offers an oasis of luxury and tranquility. The palatial property showcases elegant rooms and suites, private beaches, an indulgent spa, and an exquisite selection of restaurants and lounges. Unwind in the opulent surroundings and experience the epitome of refined Arabian hospitality.

Boutique Hotels
For travelers seeking a more intimate and personalized experience, Doha boasts a selection of boutique hotels that offer a distinctive charm, unique design, and an ambiance that reflects the local culture. These properties focus on providing personalized service and attention to detail. Consider the following boutique hotels for an exceptional stay:

The Avenue: Nestled in the vibrant West Bay area, The Avenue is a boutique hotel that combines contemporary style with Qatari hospitality. Each room is thoughtfully designed with modern comforts and a touch of local flair. Enjoy the rooftop pool, fitness center, and dine at their trendy restaurant offering a fusion of international and local flavors.

Musheireb Boutique Hotel: Situated in the heart of the Msheireb Downtown Doha project, this boutique hotel captures the essence of Qatari heritage and culture. The property seamlessly blends traditional elements with modern luxury, featuring tastefully appointed rooms, a rooftop lounge with panoramic views, and a restaurant serving authentic Qatari cuisine.

The Town Hotel Doha: Located in the bustling Al Sadd area, The Town Hotel Doha offers a cozy and charming retreat. The hotel's contemporary design is complemented by warm hospitality and personalized service. Relax in well-appointed rooms, savor international cuisine at their restaurant, and take advantage of the convenient location to explore the city's attractions.

Mid-Range Hotels
Doha caters to travelers seeking comfortable accommodations without compromising on quality or breaking the bank. These mid-range hotels provide excellent value for money, ensuring a pleasant and convenient stay. Consider the following popular mid-range options:

Holiday Inn Doha - The Business Park: Situated in the heart of Doha's business district, this modern hotel offers comfortable rooms, a fitness center, and a rooftop pool. With its convenient location, it provides easy access to major attractions, shopping malls, and the airport.

Radisson Blu Hotel: Located in the vibrant city center, Radisson Blu Hotel boasts stylish rooms, an outdoor pool, and multiple dining options. The hotel's central location allows for easy exploration of Doha's cultural sites, shopping districts, and entertainment venues.

Millennium Central Hotel Doha: Positioned in the Al Sadd area, Millennium Central Hotel Doha provides contemporary accommodation with modern amenities. The hotel features spacious rooms, a rooftop pool, a fitness center, and a variety of dining options. Its proximity to major attractions and the vibrant Souq Waqif makes it an ideal choice for travelers seeking convenience and affordability.

Budget-Friendly Stays

Traveling on a budget doesn't mean compromising on comfort or quality. Doha offers a range of budget-friendly accommodation options that provide affordability without sacrificing a pleasant stay. Consider the following properties for affordable yet comfortable stays:

La Villa Inn: Situated in the Al Mansoura area, La Villa Inn offers budget-friendly rooms with essential amenities. The hotel provides a cozy and convenient base for exploring the city, with its proximity to popular attractions, shopping centers, and restaurants.

Rawda Hotel: Located in the bustling Al Muntazah area, Rawda Hotel offers affordable rooms and suites, making it an excellent choice for budget-conscious travelers. The hotel provides a comfortable stay with convenient access to the city's main sights and entertainment options.

Kingsgate Hotel Doha: Positioned in the Al Ghanim area, Kingsgate Hotel Doha offers value-for-money accommodation with comfortable rooms and essential amenities. The hotel's central location allows guests to easily explore the city's attractions, including Souq Waqif and the Museum of Islamic Art.

When it comes to finding and booking accommodation in Doha, several popular apps and websites can help simplify the process and provide you with a range of options. Here are some widely used platforms for finding and booking accommodation in Doha:

Booking.com
Booking.com is a well-known online travel agency that offers a wide selection of hotels, apartments, and guesthouses in Doha. It provides detailed information, user reviews, and competitive pricing options. The platform allows you to filter results based on your preferences and offers a secure booking process.

Airbnb

Airbnb is a popular platform for booking unique accommodations, including apartments, villas, and rooms in Doha. It provides a more personalized experience, allowing you to connect directly with hosts and stay in local neighborhoods. Airbnb offers various filters to refine your search based on price range, amenities, and location.

Expedia

Expedia is a comprehensive travel platform that allows you to book flights, hotels, and vacation packages. It offers a wide range of accommodation options in Doha, including luxury hotels, budget-friendly stays, and boutique properties. Expedia provides user reviews, flexible booking options, and often offers package deals that combine flights and accommodation.

Agoda

Agoda is a popular platform specializing in hotel bookings and offers a wide selection of accommodations in Doha. The app features competitive pricing, exclusive deals, and allows you to search for hotels based on your preferences. Agoda provides user reviews and a user-friendly interface for easy booking.

Hotels.com

Hotels.com is another widely used platform for finding and booking hotels in Doha. It offers a comprehensive selection of accommodations, including luxury hotels, boutique properties, and budget-friendly options. The platform provides detailed hotel information, guest reviews, and loyalty programs for additional savings.

Kayak
Kayak is a travel search engine that aggregates information from various travel websites to help you find the best deals on accommodations in Doha. It allows you to compare prices, filter results based on your preferences, and provides a user-friendly interface for booking. Kayak also offers a price alert feature that notifies you when prices drop.

Tripadvisor
Tripadvisor is a popular travel website that offers user-generated reviews and ratings for hotels, restaurants, and attractions. It can be a useful resource for researching accommodations in Doha and gathering insights from other travelers' experiences. Tripadvisor provides a booking platform where you can directly book hotels based on availability.

Remember to read reviews, compare prices, and consider the location, amenities, and overall value for money when choosing your accommodation in Doha. Each platform offers its own unique features and benefits, so exploring multiple apps or websites can help you find the best option that suits your needs and preferences.

It doesn't matter if you're seeking luxury, boutique charm, mid-range comfort, or budget-friendly options,

Doha offers a diverse range of accommodations to suit every traveler's preferences and budget. From iconic luxury hotels with impeccable service to intimate boutique establishments that exude local charm, you'll find the perfect place to retreat and rejuvenate during your stay in this captivating Arabian city.

Local Transportation: Navigating Doha's Public Transit and Taxi Services

Getting around Doha is relatively convenient, thanks to its well-developed transportation system. Here's what you need to know about local transportation:

Metro

Doha Metro is a modern and efficient way to navigate the city. The metro system connects major areas of Doha, including Hamad International Airport, West Bay, and Education City. It's a cost-effective and time-saving option for exploring the city.

Doha Metro has revolutionized public transportation in the city, providing residents and visitors with a convenient and reliable mode of transportation. The metro system consists of four lines: Red Line, Gold Line, Green Line, and Blue Line, covering a total of around 85 kilometers. Each line serves different areas of Doha, ensuring comprehensive coverage of the city.

One of the key advantages of using the Doha Metro is its connectivity to major landmarks and attractions. For travelers arriving at Hamad International Airport, the Red Line provides a direct link to the city center and popular destinations. The Red Line also connects to key areas such as Souq Waqif, Msheireb Downtown, and Katara Cultural Village, making it a convenient choice for exploring cultural and entertainment hubs.

The Gold Line is particularly useful for accessing Education City, home to renowned universities and educational institutions. It offers a hassle-free commute for students, faculty, and visitors to the educational and research facilities in the area.

The Green Line connects various residential areas, commercial districts, and shopping centers, including Al Riffa, Al Mansoura, and Al Rayyan. This line is convenient for residents and commuters traveling within these areas for work or leisure.

The Doha Metro stations are equipped with modern amenities and facilities to ensure a comfortable experience for passengers. Each station features air-conditioned waiting areas, ticketing machines, and information boards displaying train timings and route maps. The stations are also designed to be accessible for people with disabilities, with ramps, elevators, and designated seating areas.

To use the Doha Metro, passengers need to purchase a reusable travel card, known as the "Karwa Smartcard." These cards can be loaded with credit for multiple journeys and can be easily topped up at vending machines available at the stations. The fares are calculated based on the distance traveled, and the card is tapped at the entry and exit gates to deduct the appropriate fare. The Karwa Smartcard can also be used for bus rides, providing a convenient integrated transportation system.

Bus

Doha's bus network covers a wide area, making it an affordable option for getting around. Mowasalat operates the bus services, and you can find information on routes, schedules, and fares on their website or at bus stops.

Doha's bus network complements the metro system, providing an extensive coverage area and serving both popular and less-frequented locations. Mowasalat, the state-owned transport company, operates the bus services in Doha. The buses are air-conditioned, comfortable, and equipped with facilities such as free Wi-Fi, ensuring a pleasant journey for passengers.

The bus routes cover a wide range of destinations, including residential areas, commercial districts, tourist attractions, and shopping centers. Whether you want to visit Aspire Zone, Villaggio Mall, or the Museum of Islamic Art, there is likely a bus route that can take you there.

To navigate the bus system effectively, it's advisable to plan your journey in advance. Mowasalat provides detailed information on routes, schedules, and fares on their official website and at bus stops. The website offers a trip planner tool that allows you to enter your origin and destination to find the most suitable bus routes and timings.

At bus stops, you'll find information boards displaying the bus numbers, routes, and estimated arrival times. The buses in Doha operate on a fixed schedule, so it's important to be aware of the timings to avoid any inconvenience.

Fares for bus rides are generally lower compared to other modes of transportation in Doha, making it a budget-friendly option for travelers. The exact fare can be paid in cash when boarding the bus, and it's advisable to carry smaller denominations for convenience. Alternatively, you can use the Karwa Smartcard, which can be tapped on the card reader as you board the bus to deduct the appropriate fare.

It's worth noting that the bus system in Doha is continuously improving and expanding. New routes are added, and adjustments to schedules are made periodically to enhance the efficiency of the service. Therefore, it's always recommended to check for any updates or changes in routes and timings before your journey.

Taxis

Taxis are readily available in Doha, and they offer a convenient way to travel, especially if you prefer door-to-door service. Both regular taxis and luxury limousines are available, and you can easily find them at taxi stands or book through mobile apps like Karwa or Uber.

Taxis are a popular mode of transportation in Doha, providing a comfortable and flexible option for getting around the city. They offer the convenience of door-to-door service, making them a preferred choice for travelers with heavy luggage or those looking for a direct commute.

In Doha, you'll find two types of taxis: regular taxis and luxury limousines. Regular taxis, often painted in maroon or orange colors, are readily available at designated taxi stands located at popular areas, including hotels, malls, and tourist attractions. Luxury limousines, on the other hand, provide a more upscale experience and can be booked in advance for specific journeys or for longer durations.

To hail a regular taxi, simply head to a taxi stand or wave at an available taxi passing by. Taxis in Doha are metered, and the fare is calculated based on distance traveled. It's important to ensure that the taxi driver starts the meter at the beginning of the journey to ensure a fair fare calculation. Tipping is not mandatory but is appreciated for good service.

For added convenience, you can also use mobile apps like Karwa or Uber to book taxis in Doha. These apps allow you to request a taxi and track its arrival in real-time. They also provide estimated fares and allow for cashless payments, providing a seamless experience for travelers.

When using taxis, it's helpful to have your destination address written down or saved on your phone in case of any language barriers. It's also recommended to carry smaller denominations of Qatari Riyals to pay for your fare, as taxi drivers may not always have change for larger bills.

In Doha, there are several popular apps that you can use to find and book transportation conveniently. These apps provide a seamless experience and offer various options for getting around the city. Here are some of the most widely used transportation apps in Doha:

Karwa
Karwa is the official taxi app in Doha. It allows you to book taxis easily and track their arrival in real-time. You can input your pickup and drop-off locations, select the type of vehicle you prefer, and pay through the app using your credit card or Karwa Smartcard. Karwa also provides fare estimates and lets you rate your ride experience.

Uber

Uber is a globally recognized ride-hailing app that operates in Doha. With Uber, you can request a ride and choose from various vehicle options, including UberX, UberSELECT, and UberXL, depending on your preferences and group size. The app provides estimated fares, driver details, and real-time tracking. Payment can be made through the app using your credit card or Uber wallet.

Careem

Careem is another popular ride-hailing app in Doha, offering a convenient way to book taxis and private cars. Similar to Uber, Careem allows you to choose different vehicle types and provides fare estimates, real-time tracking, and driver details. You can pay through the app using various payment methods, including credit cards and Careem credits.

Mowasalat

Mowasalat, the state-owned transport company in Qatar, has its own app that covers bus services in Doha. The Mowasalat app provides information on bus routes, schedules, and fares. You can plan your journey, check bus arrival times, and access real-time updates. The app also includes features such as trip planners and service alerts to help you navigate the bus system effectively.

Talixo

Talixo is a global online booking platform for private transfers and chauffeur services. It allows you to pre-book a variety of vehicles, including sedans, vans, and luxury cars. Talixo provides fixed prices for your desired routes and offers options for airport transfers, city-to-city transfers, and hourly bookings. Payment can be made securely through the app.

It's important to note that availability and specific features of these apps may vary over time. It's always a good idea to check the app stores for the most up-to-date information, read user reviews, and ensure that you download the official and trusted versions of these apps.

Using transportation apps can greatly enhance your experience in Doha, providing you with easy access to various modes of transportation and ensuring a smooth and convenient journey throughout the city.

Overall, taxis in Doha offer a reliable and convenient mode of transportation, particularly for shorter distances or when traveling with a group or heavy luggage. Whether you choose a regular taxi or opt for a luxury limousine, you can expect a comfortable and efficient ride to your desired destination.

Unique Activities and Hidden Gems in Doha

Doha offers a plethora of unique experiences and hidden gems that will make your visit truly memorable. Here are some of them and places to explore:

Souq Waqif: Immerse yourself in the vibrant atmosphere of Souq Waqif, a traditional market where you can shop for spices, textiles, and handicrafts. Indulge in authentic Qatari cuisine at the numerous restaurants and cafes, and catch a live performance at the Al Rayyan Theater.

Souq Waqif, meaning "standing market," is a bustling marketplace located in the heart of Doha. It is a place where tradition meets modernity, and visitors can experience the rich heritage of Qatar. The market has a history that dates back centuries and has been a vibrant hub of trade and commerce for locals and visitors alike.

As you step into Souq Waqif, you'll be instantly captivated by its unique charm. The narrow alleyways are filled with the scents of spices, the vibrant colors of textiles, and the sound of bargaining. It's a sensory delight that takes you on a journey through Qatari culture.

One of the highlights of Souq Waqif is its diverse array of shops and stalls. You'll find a wide range of products, including spices, perfumes, traditional garments, jewelry, and handicrafts. Take your time to explore the various stalls, interact with the friendly shopkeepers, and haggle for the best prices. The market is known for its excellent selection of spices, such as saffron, cardamom, and cinnamon, which are perfect for adding an exotic touch to your culinary adventures.

After a day of shopping, satisfy your taste buds at the numerous restaurants and cafes scattered throughout the market. Indulge in authentic Qatari cuisine, including delicious dishes like machbous (spiced rice with meat), harees (wheat and meat porridge), and luqaimat (sweet dumplings). The restaurants offer a cozy ambiance where you can relax and enjoy the local flavors while observing the lively atmosphere of the market.

For a memorable evening, head to the Al Rayyan Theater located within Souq Waqif. The theater showcases live performances, including traditional music, dance, and theater productions. Immerse yourself in the vibrant cultural scene of Qatar as talented performers take the stage and transport you into a world of artistic expression.

Al Jazeera Media Network: Take a behind-the-scenes tour of Al Jazeera, one of the world's largest news networks. Get a glimpse of how news is produced and gain insights into the media industry.

For those interested in journalism and the media industry, a visit to the Al Jazeera Media Network is a fascinating experience. Al Jazeera is one of the most prominent and influential news networks globally, known for its comprehensive coverage of news and current affairs from the Middle East and around the world.

Through a behind-the-scenes tour, visitors can gain a glimpse into the inner workings of this renowned media organization. Learn about the history and evolution of Al Jazeera, its groundbreaking approach to news reporting, and the impact it has had on the media landscape.

During the tour, you'll have the opportunity to visit the newsrooms, production studios, and control rooms, where you can observe firsthand how news is gathered, edited, and broadcasted. Engage with journalists, editors, and technical staff who play vital roles in delivering news to millions of viewers worldwide. Gain insights into the challenges and complexities of reporting on global events and learn about the ethical considerations that guide the network's journalism.

As you explore Al Jazeera, you'll come to appreciate the dedication and professionalism of the individuals working behind the scenes. They strive to provide accurate, balanced, and comprehensive news coverage, reflecting the network's commitment to journalistic integrity.

Al Khor Mangrove Forest: Escape the city and explore the serene Al Khor Mangrove Forest, located just outside Doha. Kayak through the mangroves, spot migratory birds, and discover the rich biodiversity of this unique ecosystem.

When you want to escape the bustling city and reconnect with nature, a visit to the Al Khor Mangrove Forest is a perfect choice. Located on the northern outskirts of Doha, this tranquil sanctuary offers a serene retreat and a chance to explore the unique ecosystem of mangroves.

As you enter the mangrove forest, you'll find yourself surrounded by a maze of narrow channels and dense vegetation. The mangroves serve as a vital ecosystem, acting as a natural filtration system and providing a habitat for numerous marine species and migratory birds.

To fully experience the beauty of the mangroves, embark on a kayaking adventure. Glide through the calm waters, navigating the labyrinth of channels, and marvel at the intricate root systems of the mangrove trees. As you paddle, keep an eye out for the diverse birdlife that calls the mangroves home, including herons, egrets, and flamingos. The mangroves also serve as a nursery for marine life, so if you're lucky, you might spot small fish and crabs darting beneath the water's surface.

While exploring the mangroves, take a moment to appreciate the serenity and tranquility of the surroundings. The peaceful atmosphere provides an excellent opportunity for relaxation, introspection, and connecting with nature.

Guided tours are available for those who want to learn more about the ecological significance of mangroves and the efforts to preserve and protect this delicate ecosystem. Knowledgeable guides can share insights into the various mangrove species, their importance in coastal ecosystems, and the challenges they face due to environmental factors.

Visiting the Al Khor Mangrove Forest allows you to appreciate the beauty of nature and gain a deeper understanding of the importance of preserving these fragile ecosystems for future generations.

Msheireb Museums: Visit the Msheireb Museums, which showcase Qatari culture, history, and heritage. Explore the four interconnected museums that provide an immersive experience and delve into Qatar's past.

Located in the heart of Doha, the Msheireb Museums are a collection of four interconnected museums that offer a captivating journey into Qatari culture, history, and heritage. These museums provide visitors with a comprehensive understanding of Qatar's past, present, and future, while celebrating the country's rich traditions.

Company House: Begin your exploration of the Msheireb Museums with a visit to the Company House. This museum focuses on the history and development of the Qatar Petroleum Company and its impact on the nation's growth. Explore the interactive exhibits, historical artifacts, and multimedia presentations that highlight the evolution of Qatar's oil and gas industry.

Bin Jelmood House: The Bin Jelmood House is dedicated to educating visitors about the history of slavery in Qatar and the region. Gain insights into the transatlantic slave trade, the abolition of slavery, and Qatar's role in this dark chapter of history. Engage with thought-provoking displays and exhibitions that shed light on the resilience and determination of those affected by slavery.

Mohammed Bin Jassim House: Step back in time as you enter the Mohammed Bin Jassim House, which showcases traditional Qatari architecture and the lifestyle of the Qatari elite in the 19th and early 20th centuries. Explore the beautifully restored courtyard, majlis (reception room), and living spaces adorned with intricate decorations and furnishings. Learn about the cultural customs, traditions, and social dynamics of Qatari society during this era.

Radwani House: The Radwani House offers a glimpse into the daily lives of Qatari families in the mid-20th century. Explore the rooms, including the kitchen, bedroom, and majlis, which are meticulously reconstructed to depict the lifestyle and domestic activities of that time. Discover the cultural values, familial bonds, and community spirit that shaped Qatari society during this period.

Each museum within the Msheireb Museums complex offers a unique perspective on Qatar's history and heritage. Through engaging exhibits, multimedia presentations, and interactive displays, visitors can gain a deeper appreciation for the rich cultural tapestry of the country.

Al Zubarah Archaeological Site: Embark on a journey to Al Zubarah, a UNESCO World Heritage Site that showcases the remains of an ancient Qatari town. Explore the archaeological site, visit the museum, and learn about the region's fascinating history.

Located approximately 100 kilometers northwest of Doha, Al Zubarah Archaeological Site is a UNESCO World Heritage Site that stands as a testament to Qatar's rich historical legacy. This well-preserved archaeological site offers a captivating glimpse into the ancient town of Al Zubarah, which flourished during the 18th and 19th centuries.

As you explore the site, you'll discover the remnants of a once-thriving pearl fishing and trading port. The ruins provide valuable insights into the town's urban layout, architecture, and way of life during its heyday. Walk through the streets and alleyways, and marvel at the remains of houses, mosques, defensive structures, and commercial buildings. The mudbrick fortifications that surround the town are particularly impressive and highlight the strategic importance of Al Zubarah in its time.

To further enhance your understanding of the site, a visit to the Al Zubarah Archaeological Site Museum is highly recommended. The museum showcases a vast collection of artifacts unearthed from the site, including pottery, jewelry, weaponry, and navigational instruments. These artifacts provide valuable insights into the economic, social, and cultural aspects of life in Al Zubarah.

The museum also offers interactive displays, multimedia presentations, and informative exhibits that shed light on the historical context of the town. Learn about the significance of pearl diving, the trading routes that connected Al Zubarah with the Arabian Gulf and beyond, and the cultural exchange that took place in this cosmopolitan hub.

Exploring Al Zubarah and its museum is a journey back in time, allowing you to appreciate the legacy of Qatar's maritime history and the important role played by Al Zubarah in the region's trade and cultural connections.

Desert Safari: Experience the thrill of a desert safari by venturing into Qatar's stunning sand dunes. Take a thrilling ride on a 4x4 vehicle, try sandboarding, enjoy a camel ride, and witness a mesmerizing desert sunset.

A visit to Qatar is incomplete without experiencing the exhilaration of a desert safari. The country's vast expanse of golden sand dunes offers an ideal setting for an unforgettable adventure in the desert.

One of the most popular activities during a desert safari is a thrilling ride on a 4x4 vehicle. Skilled drivers will take you on a rollercoaster-like journey through the towering dunes, navigating steep slopes and sharp turns. Feel your adrenaline surge as the vehicle glides over the sand, providing an exhilarating and heart-pounding experience.

For the adventurous souls, sandboarding is a must-try activity. Strap on a sandboard, stand atop a dune, and slide down the slopes, feeling the rush of excitement as you carve your way through the soft sand. Whether you're a beginner or an experienced sandboarder, the dunes of Qatar offer endless possibilities for adrenaline-fueled fun.

To truly immerse yourself in the desert experience, enjoy a camel ride across the picturesque dunes. Feel the gentle sway of the camel's gait as you traverse the sandy terrain, allowing yourself to be transported back in time to the days of old when camels were the primary means of transportation across the desert.

As the day draws to a close, prepare to be mesmerized by the breathtaking sight of a desert sunset. Witness the vibrant colors of the sky as the sun sinks below the horizon, casting a golden glow over the vast desert landscape. Capture this magical moment with your camera or simply take a moment to absorb the beauty and tranquility of the desert.

Throughout your desert safari, you'll have opportunities to learn about the desert ecosystem, its flora and fauna, and the traditional Bedouin way of life. Knowledgeable guides will share interesting insights into the desert's significance in Qatari culture and history, as well as its importance in preserving the natural heritage of the region.

Katara Cultural Village: Immerse yourself in Qatar's cultural scene at Katara Cultural Village. Explore art galleries, attend live performances, visit the amphitheater, and indulge in delicious international cuisine at the various restaurants.

Nestled along the coastline of Doha, Katara Cultural Village is a vibrant hub that celebrates arts, culture, and heritage from around the world. It is a cultural oasis where visitors can immerse themselves in a diverse range of artistic expressions, attend captivating performances, and indulge in culinary delights.

Art enthusiasts will find themselves captivated by the art galleries that showcase both local and international artwork. Discover contemporary exhibitions, traditional Qatari art, and thought-provoking installations that provide insights into various artistic styles and themes. From paintings and sculptures to multimedia displays, the galleries at Katara Cultural Village offer a rich tapestry of artistic expression.

For those seeking live performances, the village's amphitheater is a prime destination. It hosts a wide array of shows, including theater productions, music concerts, dance performances, and cultural festivals. Be enchanted by the melodic tunes of local musicians, marvel at the grace and precision of traditional dance troupes, and witness the fusion of global artistic influences on the stage.

Katara Cultural Village is also a culinary haven, offering a wide range of dining options to tantalize your taste buds. Indulge in delicious international cuisine at the various restaurants, cafes, and food stalls scattered throughout the village. From traditional Qatari dishes to flavors from around the globe, there's something to satisfy every palate. Whether you're craving a lavish fine dining experience or a quick bite to eat, Katara Cultural Village has an array of options to suit your preferences.

As you stroll through the village, you'll be captivated by the stunning architecture that combines traditional Qatari elements with contemporary design. The intricate details, ornate facades, and beautiful waterfront views create a picturesque setting that enhances the overall cultural experience.

Katara Cultural Village is not just a place to visit; it's a place to engage, appreciate, and celebrate the diverse cultures that shape the world. It provides a platform for cultural exchange, fostering dialogue and understanding among people from different backgrounds.

In Conclusion, Doha offers a plethora of experiences and attractions for travelers seeking a blend of rich history, cultural immersion, and thrilling adventures. From exploring vibrant markets like Souq Waqif and diving into the ancient past at Al Zubarah Archaeological Site to embracing the natural beauty of the Al Khor Mangrove Forest and experiencing the excitement of a desert safari, Doha has something to offer every visitor. Additionally, the Msheireb Museums provide an opportunity to delve into Qatar's culture and heritage, while a visit to Al Jazeera offers unique insights into the world of media. Finally, Katara Cultural Village allows travelers to immerse themselves in a diverse range of artistic expressions, live performances, and culinary delights. Embrace the charm and allure of Doha as you embark on a journey that will leave you with lasting memories of this captivating city.

Remember, these are just a few of the countless experiences and hidden gems that await you in Doha. Don't be afraid to venture off the beaten path and discover your own unique adventures in this captivating city.

CHAPTER EIGHT

19 TO DO LIST FOR AN UNFORGETTABLE EXPERIENCE IN DOHA

Doha offers a multitude of experiences that will leave you in awe. To ensure you make the most of your time in this dynamic city, here is a curated list of 19 must-do activities for the full memorable Doha experience It doesn't matter if you're a history buff, a food enthusiast, or an adventure seeker, this to-do list will guide you through a memorable journey in Doha, where tradition meets innovation and surprises await at around every corner.

1. **Marvel at the architectural wonders of the modern skyline, including the iconic Burj Qatar and Aspire Tower**

    - Take a leisurely walk or drive around Doha's city center to witness the impressive skyline dominated by towering architectural masterpieces.

    - Admire the Burj Qatar, also known as the Tornado Tower, with its striking spiral design that symbolizes Qatar's rapid development.

- Visit the Aspire Tower, a majestic structure that houses a hotel and an observation deck offering panoramic views of Doha.

2. **Explore the traditional charm of Souq Waqif, a bustling marketplace filled with vibrant stalls and authentic Qatari products**

- Immerse yourself in the sights, sounds, and scents of this traditional Qatari souq, which has been restored to its former glory.

- Browse through the narrow alleyways and discover a wide array of goods, including spices, textiles, jewelry, and traditional handicrafts.

- Enjoy a cup of aromatic Qatari coffee or indulge in a traditional meal at one of the many restaurants serving local delicacies.

3. **Visit the Museum of Islamic Art and immerse yourself in the world of Islamic art and culture**

- Marvel at the stunning architecture of the museum, designed by I.M. Pei, and its picturesque location on an artificial island.

- Explore the extensive collection of Islamic art, including ancient manuscripts, ceramics, metalwork, textiles, and jewelry.

- Attend educational programs, workshops, or lectures offered by the museum to gain a deeper understanding of Islamic art and its significance.

4. **Take a stroll along the Doha Corniche and enjoy breathtaking views of the city's skyline and the Arabian Gulf**

- Enjoy a leisurely walk or rent a bike to explore the scenic Corniche, a waterfront promenade stretching several kilometers.

- Take in the panoramic views of Doha's modern skyline, dotted with towering skyscrapers and architectural marvels.

- Relax on one of the many well-maintained parks along the Corniche or indulge in a picnic while enjoying the gentle sea breeze.

5. **Indulge in a desert safari adventure, where you can go dune bashing, camel riding, and experience the beauty of Qatar's desert landscapes**

- Embark on an exhilarating desert safari tour, where skilled drivers take you on a thrilling ride over the sandy dunes.

- Try your hand at sandboarding or experience the traditional mode of transportation by riding a camel through the desert.

- Witness a mesmerizing desert sunset and enjoy a traditional Bedouin-style dinner under the starlit sky, complete with cultural performances.

6. **Discover the history of Qatar at the National Museum of Qatar, an architectural masterpiece that tells the story of the country's past**

- Explore the unique structure of the National Museum, designed by Jean Nouvel, which resembles a desert rose.

- Journey through interactive exhibits, multimedia presentations, and artifacts that showcase the history, culture, and natural heritage of Qatar.

- Visit the Heritage Library within the museum to delve deeper into the country's archival materials, manuscripts, and rare books.

7. **Explore the Katara Cultural Village, a hub for arts, music, and cultural events showcasing Qatar's creative spirit**

- Wander through the beautifully designed cultural village that hosts art exhibitions, music concerts, and theatrical performances.

- Visit the galleries and art spaces to appreciate the works of local and international artists, showcasing a diverse range of art forms.

- Attend cultural festivals and events held throughout the year, celebrating music, film, literature, and performing arts from around the world.

8. Embark on a dhow cruise along the coastline of Doha, enjoying stunning views and a delicious traditional meal

- Board a traditional wooden dhow boat and set sail along the Doha Bay, taking in the breathtaking views of the city skyline and the sparkling waters.

- Indulge in a delectable Qatari meal served on board, featuring local specialties like mezze, grilled meats, and seafood dishes.

- Sit back, relax, and enjoy the gentle breeze as you soak up the tranquil atmosphere and admire the city from a different perspective.

9. **Experience the thrill of indoor skydiving at iFLY Doha, where you can defy gravity in a safe and controlled environment**

   - Try the exhilarating experience of indoor skydiving at iFLY Doha, a state-of-the-art facility that offers a simulated free-fall experience.

   - Under the guidance of experienced instructors, you can float on a cushion of air within a vertical wind tunnel, providing the sensation of skydiving.

   - No prior skydiving experience or parachute is required, making it a thrilling and accessible adventure for all ages.

10. **Shop till you drop at the luxurious malls of Doha, including Villaggio Mall and The Pearl-Qatar, home to high-end brands and designer boutiques**

    - Discover a shopper's paradise in Doha, with an array of upscale malls offering a mix of international and local brands.

    - Explore Villaggio Mall, an Italian-themed shopping destination with an indoor canal and a replica of Venice's St. Mark's Square.

    - Visit The Pearl-Qatar, an artificial island with a sophisticated ambiance, featuring luxury boutiques, waterfront promenades, and dining options.

11. Visit the falcon market and witness the Qatari tradition of falconry, an ancient practice deeply rooted in the country's heritage

- Explore the Falcon Souq, a unique market where falcon enthusiasts can purchase, train, and care for these majestic birds.

- Observe falcon trainers demonstrating the art of falconry, a traditional practice that has been passed down through generations.

- Gain insights into the importance of falcons in Qatari culture and the deep bond between falconry and the desert lifestyle.

12. Enjoy a traditional Qatari meal at one of the many authentic restaurants in Doha, savoring delicious dishes like machbous and harees

- Treat your taste buds to a culinary journey of Qatari cuisine, characterized by rich flavors and aromatic spices.

- Sample traditional dishes such as machbous (spiced rice with meat or fish), harees (slow-cooked wheat and meat), and thareed (stew with bread).

- Experience warm Qatari hospitality as you dine in restaurants that showcase traditional Qatari decor and offer a cultural ambiance.

13. Discover the underwater world at the Qatar National Aquarium, home to a diverse range of marine species

- Explore the wonders of the ocean at the Qatar National Aquarium, housing a variety of marine life, including sharks, rays, and colorful fish.

- Walk through the underwater tunnel and observe the marine creatures swimming overhead, providing an immersive and educational experience.

- Learn about marine conservation efforts and the importance of preserving Qatar's delicate coastal ecosystems.

14. Learn about Qatar's rich pearl diving history at the Al Zubarah UNESCO World Heritage Site, an archaeological site showcasing the country's maritime heritage

- Visit the Al Zubarah Archaeological Site, a UNESCO World Heritage Site that offers insights into Qatar's maritime past and the pearl diving industry.

- Explore the well-preserved ruins of the fortified town, including palaces, houses, and a mosque, providing a glimpse into the region's history.

- Learn about the techniques and challenges of pearl diving, a trade that once played a significant role in Qatar's economy.

15. Immerse yourself in the beauty of the Al Thakira Mangroves, where you can kayak through serene waterways and spot unique wildlife

- Experience the tranquility of the Al Thakira Mangroves, a pristine natural habitat located north of Doha.

- Embark on a kayak or paddleboarding adventure through the mangrove forests, observing a diverse array of bird species and other wildlife.

- Marvel at the unique ecosystem of mangroves, which provide a vital breeding ground for marine life and contribute to coastal protection.

16. Catch a live performance at the Qatar National Theatre or the Qatar Philharmonic Orchestra, witnessing the country's vibrant arts scene

- Immerse yourself in the cultural richness of Qatar by attending a live performance at the Qatar National Theatre.

- Enjoy theatrical productions, dance performances, or music concerts that showcase local and international talent.

- Alternatively, experience the symphonic delights of the Qatar Philharmonic Orchestra, which regularly performs classical and contemporary compositions.

17. Attend a traditional Qatari festival, such as the Katara International Arabian Horse Festival or the Qatari Traditional Dhow Festival, to experience local customs and traditions

- Immerse yourself in Qatari traditions and celebrations by attending one of the many cultural festivals held throughout the year.

- Witness the elegance and beauty of Arabian horses at the Katara International Arabian Horse Festival, featuring show jumping and equestrian competitions.

- Experience the Qatari Traditional Dhow Festival, celebrating the country's seafaring heritage with dhow races, traditional music, and dancing.

18. Relax and unwind at one of Doha's luxurious spas, indulging in rejuvenating treatments inspired by ancient Arabian rituals

- Pamper yourself with a spa day at one of Doha's renowned wellness retreats, offering a range of indulgent treatments and therapies.

- Experience traditional hammam rituals, soothing massages, and revitalizing skincare treatments, all designed to promote relaxation and well-being.

- Allow the expert therapists to transport you to a state of bliss as they draw upon ancient Arabian techniques and natural ingredients.

19. Take a day trip to the stunning inland sea of Khor Al Adaid, where you can witness the meeting of the desert and the sea in a breathtaking natural setting

- Embark on an unforgettable journey to Khor Al Adaid, also known as the Inland Sea, located in the southeastern part of Qatar.

- Marvel at the unique phenomenon where the sea flows into the heart of the desert, creating a stunning landscape of rolling sand dunes and tranquil waters.

- Enjoy activities such as dune bashing, sandboarding, or simply relax by the seaside, taking in the beauty of this natural wonder.

From architectural marvels and cultural encounters to thrilling adventures and tranquil escapes, Doha offers a diverse range of attractions and activities that cater to every traveler's interests.

CONCLUSION

As you reach the end of this comprehensive travel guide, you have undoubtedly delved deep into the captivating essence of Doha, the jewel of the Arabian Peninsula. Throughout your journey, you have experienced the perfect blend of tradition and modernity, where the rich tapestry of Qatari culture seamlessly intertwines with the glimmering marvels of a modern metropolis. It is here, in Doha, that ancient customs harmoniously coexist with contemporary wonders, leaving an indelible mark on all who venture into its embrace.

Doha, with its iconic landmarks, has taken you on a remarkable voyage of discovery. From the opulent Pearl-Qatar, where luxury, art, and entertainment converge, to the bustling Souq Waqif, where authentic flavors and vibrant ambiance awaken your senses, each corner of this city reveals a unique story. The Katara Cultural Village has transported you back in time, immersing you in the artistic and cultural heritage of Qatar, while the Museum of Islamic Art has dazzled you with its exquisite collection of timeless artifacts. And as you strolled along the Corniche, the picturesque promenade etched with the city's skyline, you witnessed the undeniable allure of Doha in all its glory.

But Doha is more than just its landmarks; it is a gateway to a world steeped in tradition and culture. You have gained insights into Qatari customs and etiquette, unlocking a deeper understanding of the local way of life. The celebration of Qatar National Day has filled you with a sense of national pride and unity, as you joined in the festivities and witnessed the spirit of independence that resonates throughout the country. And of course, you have indulged in the tantalizing flavors of traditional Qatari cuisine, savoring the rich blend of spices and culinary delights that define this region.

Beyond the borders of Doha, you embarked on thrilling day trips, exploring the vastness of the desert and unearthing the remnants of Qatar's ancient history at the Al Zubarah Archaeological Site. The Umm Salal Mohammed Fort offered a glimpse into Qatari heritage, transporting you to a time long gone. And as you immersed yourself in the breathtaking natural wonders surrounding Doha, you found solace in the serenity of Aspire Park, reveled in the sun, sand, and sea at Sealine Beach Resort, and marveled at the diverse ecosystem of the Mangrove Forests in Al Thakira.

Doha's modern marvels have left an indelible mark on your journey. The Education City, with its cutting-edge learning and innovation, has showcased Qatar's commitment to shaping the future. Lusail City, a futuristic urban development project, has provided a glimpse into what lies ahead, while Qanat Quartier on The Pearl-Qatar has transported you to a Mediterranean-inspired haven amidst the Arabian Peninsula.

Let us not forget the vibrant shopping and entertainment experiences that awaits in Doha. From retail therapy at Villaggio Mall to the dynamic blend of shopping, dining, and entertainment at Doha Festival City, this city caters to every desire. And as night falls, the vibrant bars, clubs, and cultural performances come alive, offering a taste of Doha's vibrant nightlife.

Armed with practical tips and recommendations, you are now equipped to navigate this enchanting city with ease. Whether you choose to indulge in luxurious accommodations, seek budget-friendly options, or venture off the beaten path to discover hidden gems, Doha has something for everyone.

As you reflect on your Arabian Peninsula adventure, the allure of Doha lingers in your heart. It is a place where ancient traditions intertwine with modern aspirations, where a deep-rooted culture coexists harmoniously with innovation and progress. Doha has cast its spell on you, leaving you with unforgettable memories and a longing to return.

So, embrace the allure of Doha and let its captivating embrace guide you through an extraordinary journey of exploration, culture, and adventure. Discover the riches of the Arabian Peninsula and immerse yourself in the wonders of this modern oasis. Your ultimate handbook to Doha has paved the way for an experience like no other. Unveil the magic, embark on the adventure, and let Doha captivate you with its undeniable allure.

ON A FINAL NOTE

The information provided in this travel guide is intended for general informational purposes as diligent effort has been made to ensure the accuracy of the information provided. Readers are solely responsible for their own travel decisions and activities and should use their judgment when following the suggestions and recommendations provided in this guide. Note that prices, hours of operation, and other details are subject to change without notice. It is always advisable to check with the relevant authorities, businesses, or organizations before making any travel plans or reservations.

The inclusion of any specific product, service, business, or organization in this guide does not constitute an endorsement by the author. Readers are advised to take necessary precautions and follow local laws, regulations, and customs. The author and publisher of this travel guide are not responsible for any inaccuracies or omissions, nor for any damages or losses that may result from following the information provided in this guide.

Thank you for choosing this DOHA TRAVEL GUIDE, and bon voyage!

MY TRAVEL NOTES

....

....

....

....

....

....

....

....

....

....

....

....

Printed in Great Britain
by Amazon

28755965R00126